THE Hitler FILE

THE ESSENTIAL FACTS

THE Hitler FILE

THE ESSENTIAL FACTS

PATRICK DELAFORCE

MICHAEL O'MARA BOOKS LIMITED

For Gillian

First published in Great Britain in 2007 by
Michael O'Mara Books Limited
9 Lion Yard, Tremadoc Road
London sw4 7nq

A CIP catalogue record for this book is available
from the British Library

Papers used by Michael O'Mara Books Limited are natural,
recyclable products made from wood grown in sustainable
forests. The manufacturing processes conform to the
environmental regulations of the country of origin.

ISBN: 978-1-84317-244-4

1 3 5 7 9 10 8 6 4 2

www.mombooks.com

Designed and typeset by Martin Bristow

Printed and bound in Finland by WS Bookwell, Juva

INTRODUCTION

ONE OF THE GREATEST MYSTERIES of the twentieth century is how a motley collection of not very intelligent German street brawlers, led and totally dominated by one man, could by brutal war take most of Europe and threaten the rest of the world. Adolf Hitler (1889–1945), an Austrian 'misfit' and loner, with a slight education, no family genes of note and no political background, created the infamous Third Reich by sheer determination, confidence, willpower and luck.

Whilst in Landsberg prison in 1923–24, guilty of a premature, badly planned attempt to seize power in Bavaria, Hitler composed a long, boring diatribe that he called *Mein Kampf* (*My Struggle*); it sold seven million copies. The book told the world, *inter alia*, of his ruthless plans to seize power and smash and grab much of Europe and Russia to obtain *Lebensraum* – more living space – for eighty million Germans. But the world did not pay attention. Those who managed to read through the turgid pages of arrogant self-justification were either of the same mind or just could not envisage a thirty-four-year-old rabble-rouser actually clawing his way to power and ultimately causing over fifty million deaths.

Although when he was stony-broke in Vienna, his vapid, prolific watercolour paintings were sold by Jewish merchants, and he himself was not sure whether his father's father was a Jew, Hitler developed a manic compulsion to destroy all the Jews in Germany, indeed in Europe. He and his terrible cohorts, among them Himmler, Goebbels, Heydrich and Eichmann, controlled thirty extermination centres for the implementation of the 'Final Solution' – the wholesale destruction of European Jewry. In

Mein Kampf Hitler set out his belief in the superiority of Aryan and Nordic races, and the international conspiracy by the Jews, whom he believed were using even Bolshevism, particularly Russian Bolshevism, to achieve world domination.

The power of his personality, drive, zeal, iron will, eternal optimism and promises of peace had an immense impact. In the early 1930s he convinced his National Socialist German Workers' Party (all other parties had been outlawed) and his supporters that the new Germany, Nazi Germany, under his leadership as Führer (leader) was great, was strong and had a manifest destiny, even though there would be sacrifices along the way. In April 1939, Hitler wrote to the American President Roosevelt, 'I took over a state which was faced by complete ruin [after the Weimar Republic], thanks to its trust in the promises of the rest of the world . . . I have conquered chaos in Germany, re-established order and enormously increased production . . . I have succeeded in finding useful work for the seven million unemployed . . .'

And it is true that in terms of social reform, there was much that was good – or at least beneficial to the (non-Jewish) German population. There are many examples of Hitler's social reforms: vast improvements in workers' conditions, at work and at home; benevolent farming laws; laws for the reduction of unemployment; the establishment of chambers of culture; the building of autobahns; the Volkswagen; workers' recreation facilities; the 'Strength through Joy' movement; and holiday courses. Through Goebbels he controlled all the media in Germany and with his compelling oratory simply brainwashed the German people over a twelve-year period. His people regarded him as 'The Messiah', the German women adored him and the men, including the other Nazi leaders, feared him.

He was to become hated and feared throughout the world, and seen by many as an embodiment of evil. His beliefs, his policies, his actions were vile, horrible and – yes – evil . . . but as an individual, he can be seen not as awe-inspiring but as repellent, ridiculous, pathetic, pompous, even laughable – as well as hateful. Much of this book is devoted to the background and the little details that made up this twisted individual: Hitler's schooling, academic reports, masters and choir singing; the 'loner' down-and-out in Vienna; his thwarted ambition to be a painter; his service in the Great War; his leather shorts; his *Kampf*; the first crude, amateurish, post-war efforts at demagogue politics; his loyalty to his early street thugs; his love affairs; the men and women he surrounded himself with, including two of the Mitford girls and the Duke and Duchess of Windsor; his diet; his blue eyes; the occasional brutal plot and conspiracy; and those strange final weeks in the bunker beneath the garden of the Reich Chancellery in Berlin.

Hitler once said, 'The victor in war is he who commits the fewest number of mistakes and who has, also, a blind faith in victory.' He was arrogant and ruthless – and he certainly had blind faith in victory until the dramatic events in the bunker in late April 1945 when the Russian shells were falling around him, and the end was staring him in the face.

PICTURE CREDITS

The following images are reproduced with the kind permission of the British Cartoon Archive, University of Kent and Solo Syndication/ Associated Newspapers:

Page 25: David Low, *The Evening Standard*, 18 April 1944;
page 41: David Low, *The Evening Standard*, 9 March 1933;
page 57: David Low, *The Evening Standard*, 1 March 1933;
page 69: David Low, *The Evening Standard*, 1 May 1934;
page 94: Wyndham Robinson, *The Star*, between 1 January 1937 and 31 December 1945;
page 125: David Low, *The Evening Standard*, 8 July 1936;
page 141: David Low, *The Evening Standard*, 30 May 1941;
page 171: David Low, *The Evening Standard*, 25 August 1944;
page 188: David Low, *The Evening Standard*, 2 January 1945.

The following images are reproduced with the kind permission of the National Library of Wales, Aberystwyth and Solo Syndication/ Associated Newspapers:

Page 117: Leslie Illingworth, *The Daily Mail*, 10 November 1939;
page 158: Leslie Illingworth, *The Daily Mail*, 10 February 1943.

ACKNOWLEDGEMENTS

Quotations from *Hitler's Table Talk* by François Genoud, edited by Hugh Trevor-Roper, reproduced by kind permission of Weidenfeld & Nicolson, a division of the Orion Publishing Group.

The Peasant Background

THE EMPEROR FRANZ JOSEF had ruled the still great Habsburg Empire for forty years when Adolf Hitler was born on 20 April 1889 in the small frontier town of Braunau on the River Inn. That region between the River Danube and the Bohemian border, known as the Waldviertel, with villages such as Spital, Walterschlag, Weitra, Dollersheim and Strones, had since the early fifteenth century produced families named Hüttler, Hiedler and Hitler. Possibly Czech in origin, the variously spelled name means 'smallholder', which is exactly what these families were. It was a poor region of hills and woods with a peasant population that often intermarried, with a dash of incest. It was far removed from the glittering Austrian cities.

The Pompous, Portly Father

FOR A VARIETY OF REASONS in January 1877 an officer in the Imperial Customs Service called Alois Schicklgruber (1837–1903) changed his name to Alois Hitler. From 1855 for forty years Alois served in various towns in Upper Austria, including Braunau. Photographs show him portly and pompous, in a smart uniform with glittering buttons, with the cautious face of a minor government official. He was a strange, unlikeable man who married three times and moved house eleven times in twenty-five years. Adolf was the third child of Alois's third marriage – to Klara Pölzi (1860–1907), who was twenty-three years younger than her husband. She came from the village of Spital, where the Hitlers originated, and was the granddaughter of Johan Nepomuk Hiedler (1807–88), in whose house Alois had been brought up as a child (his mother, Maria Schicklgruber, having married Hiedler's brother Johan Georg when Alois was almost five years old).

The Hitler household consisted of Alois and Klara, two children from a previous marriage – Alois junior and Angela – Adolf, Edmund and sister Paula, plus a cook and maid, and Adolf's ill-tempered, hunchbacked aunt Johanna. It was a comfortable, middle-class establishment; Alois – the provincial civil servant – was status-conscious, humourless, thrifty, very bad-tempered, smoked far too much, drank rather a lot and his main passion was bee-keeping. A legacy in 1889 from his uncle Johan Nepomuk Hiedler enabled him to buy a property in Spital. When Alois retired in 1895 at the age of fifty-eight the family moved to Hafeld-ma-Traun, then to Lambach before settling at Leonding just outside Linz, overlooking the Rivers Danube and Traun. The town of Linz became Adolf Hitler's 'spiritual' home.

The Young Choirboy

IN THE FAMOUS old Benedictine monastery in Lambach, the six-year-old Adolf Hitler served as an acolyte and choirboy and recalled 'the opportunity to intoxicate myself with the solemn splendour of the brilliant church festivals'. Later, on Whit Sunday 1904, he was confirmed in the Roman Catholic cathedral at Linz at his mother Klara's wish; she hoped her son would become a monk. Adolf adored his mother and when she died of cancer on 21 December 1907 he was desolate and wept bitterly.

'A Very Painful Adolescence'

ADOLF SPENT FIVE YEARS in primary school and in September 1900, aged eleven, entered the *Realschule* in Linz. This secondary school trained boys for a commercial or technical career. In *Mein Kampf* he wrote, 'I did not want to become a civil servant, no, and again no. All attempt on my father's part to inspire me with love or pleasure in this profession by stories from his own life accomplished the exact opposite . . . one day it became clear to me that I would become a painter, an artist . . . my father for the moment was struck speechless . . . "Artist, no, never as long as I live!"' His was, Hitler wrote, a 'very painful adolescence'.

The Very Young Political Revolutionary

WHEN HITLER, aged thirty-four, dictated *Mein Kampf* in Landsberg prison he wrote of his schoolboy life and activities. He claimed that his 'habit of historical thinking which I thus learned in school' and the study of 'world history' gave him 'an inexhaustible source of understanding . . . for politics'. 'Thus at an early age I had become a political revolutionary and I became an artistic revolutionary at an equally early age.' When he was twelve he saw a stage performance of *Wilhelm Tell* and, at thirteen, his first opera, *Lohengrin*, by Wagner. 'My youthful enthusiasm for the master of Bayreuth knew no bounds.'

The Violent Schoolboy Orator

IN *Mein Kampf* Hitler wrote, 'All my playing about in the open, the long walk to school, and particularly my association with extremely "husky" boys, which caused my mother bitter anguish, made me the very opposite of a stay-at-home . . . even then my oratorical talent was being developed in the form of more or less violent arguments with my schoolmates. I had become a little ringleader; at school I learned easily and at that time very well, but was otherwise rather hard to handle.'

His mostly rather second-rate school reports (see pages 13 and 14) do not entirely support this statement.

Hitler's Teachers

DR LEONARD PÖTSCH, an ardent German nationalist and a town councillor of Linz, taught the young Adolf Hitler history at the *Realschule*, and made a deep impression on him. 'On occasions we sat there, often aflame with enthusiasm, and sometimes even moved to tears. The national fervour which we felt in our small way was used by him as an instrument in our education. It was because I had such a professor that history became my favourite subject.' Certainly Hitler told his table companions dozens of historical titbits – he had an astonishing memory for trivia of every possible kind. Pötsch was the only teacher for whom Hitler had any respect – the others he thought absolute tyrants. 'They had no sympathy with youth; their one object was to stuff our brains and to turn us into erudite apes like themselves. If any pupil showed the slightest trace of originality, they persecuted him relentlessly.' The physics master, König, was a 'real fool'. His pupils made cruel fun of the tubby little priest who taught divinity. Hitler's French teacher had 'a frowsty beard . . . a collar . . . greasy and yellow with dirt, and he was in every way a most repellent creature . . . furious because I learnt not a word of French.'

Hitler the Poet (1)

LODGING WITH A FAMILY in Steyr in Austria, where he was then at school, Hitler, aged fifteen, spent much of his time drawing, painting and reading. He also wrote a rather deranged poem, which is now in the Bundesarchiv Koblenz. Some of the wording is not decipherable. Translated, it reads:

> The people sit there in a ventilated house
> Filling themselves with beer and wine

Eating and drinking ecstatically
(–) out then on all fours.
There they climb high mountain peaks
(–) with faces full of pride
And fall down like acrobats somersaulting
And cannot find balance
Then, sad, they return home
And quite forget the time
Then he sees (–), his wife, poor man,
Who cures his injuries with a good hiding.

The budding painter illustrated his poem with a drawing of a man being beaten by a buxom woman.

The Young Warmonger

'Rummaging through my father's library, I had come across various books of a military nature, among them a popular edition of the Franco-German War of 1870–71. It consisted of two issues of an illustrated periodical from those years, which now became my favourite reading matter,' Hitler wrote in *Mein Kampf*. 'It was not long before the great heroic struggle had become my greatest inner experience. From then on I became more and more enthusiastic about everything that was in any way connected with war or, for that matter, with soldiering.' So the Franco-Prussian War set the young Adolf on a long, long trail of military adventures. His contempt for France was probably born then.

Education, Education, Education!

HITLER'S SCHOOL REPORT for the fourth class of the school in Steyr, issued on 16 September 1905, reads:

	FIRST SEMESTER	SECOND SEMESTER
Moral conduct	Satisfactory	Satisfactory
Diligence	Unequal	Adequate
Religion	Adequate	Satisfactory
German language	Inadequate	Adequate
Geography & History	Adequate	Satisfactory
Mathematics	Inadequate	Satisfactory
Chemistry	Adequate	Adequate
Physics	Satisfactory	Adequate
Geometry	Adequate	Adequate
Freehand drawing	Laudable	Excellent
Gymnastics	Excellent	Excellent
Stenography	Inadequate	—
Singing	—	Satisfactory
Written work	Displeasing	Displeasing

The sixteen-year-old was obviously lazy (see Diligence), but performed very well in his art classes (Freehand drawing). Hitler's devotion to the history teacher at his previous school, Dr Pötsch, is not reflected in this report, whereas his 'Excellent' in gymnastics is most surprising: Hitler as an adult detested physical exercise, rarely walked and certainly played no sports.

'Notoriously Cantankerous'

IN DECEMBER 1923, following Hitler's trial for his Munich Beer Hall putsch of that November, Dr Eduard Hümer, another teacher at the *Realschule*, gave this description of the young schoolboy: 'I can recall the gaunt, pale-faced youth pretty well ... [he] had definite talent, though in a narrow field. But he lacked self-discipline, being notoriously cantankerous, wilful, arrogant and bad-tempered. He had obvious difficulty in fitting in at school. Moreover he was lazy. His enthusiasm for hard work evaporated all too quickly. He reacted with ill-concealed hostility to advice or reproof. At the same time he demanded of his fellow pupils their unqualified subservience, fancying himself in the role of leader.'

'Wholly to Art'

WHEN HE WAS SIXTEEN, Hitler's widowed mother moved with Hitler's aunt Johanna Pölzl and Paula, his sister, into an apartment in Linz, which they shared with the inadequate, arrogant dreamer, who for a time devoted himself 'wholly to art'. He sketched, painted, drew plans for museums, a bridge over the river Danube, theatres and indeed the total rebuilding of Linz. He also took piano lessons – briefly; he got bored. He became a *boulevardier* fop with a black, ivory-topped cane, and visited concerts, theatres, a musical club, a library club and a wax museum. He had one friend, August Kubizek, known as 'Gustl', who was a decorator's son, but was a drifter in a dream world, describing himself as a 'loner'.

Hitler as Playwright

IN 1906 HITLER, busy doing nothing very much whilst in Linz, was allowed to use a well-equipped library owned by the father of a friend (a government official). He discovered Richard Wagner's prose writings, including *Jews in Music* and *Decay and Regeneration*. He also went to a meeting for 'persons physically separated' (since neither religious nor civil divorce existed in Austria), and became a member of this organization. He was 'seized with virtuous indignation' on hearing of 'men who were models of ignomy, and whose wives, by law, could never separate from them,' so young Adolf Hitler decided to write a play on the subject. 'Since my writing was illegible, I dictated the play to my sister, pacing up and down in my room. The play was divided into a number of scenes. I displayed a lofty, burning imagination. At that time I was fifteen years old. My sister said to me, "You know, Adolf, your play can't be acted." I couldn't persuade her that she was mistaken.' His half-sister, Angela, 'went on strike, and that was the end of my masterpiece.'

The Artist Manqué

HITLER TRIED HARD to attend the Academy of Fine Arts in Vienna. When he registered with the Vienna police it was as a 'student', then as a 'painter' and 'studying to be a writer'. To gain admission to the Academy's school of painting he had to submit a number of his drawings. If they were considered to be reasonable, the candidate then had to take an examination in drawing, held each year in October. He was refused entry on two occasions.

1907–8

Composition exercises in drawing. First day: expulsion from paradise, etc. Second day: episode from the deluge, etc. . . .
The following took the test with insufficient results, or were not admitted: . . . Adolf Hitler, Braunau a. Inn, April 20, 1889, German, Catholic. Father civil servant. 4 classes in Realschule. Few heads. Test drawing unsatisfactory.

And in 1908

The following gentlemen performed their test drawings with insufficient success or were not admitted to the test . . . .
Adolf Hitler, Braunau a. Inn, Twentieth of April, 1889, German, Catholic, civil servant. 4 Realschulein. Not admitted to the test.

The drawings he had brought to the assessment were regarded by the examiners as being inadequate – hence no test. Hitler's version of events was that he appealed and was told that he should apply for admission to the Architectural School, but as Hitler had no high-school diploma he could not apply.

The Impoverished Orphan?

ON 29 NOVEMBER 1921, aged thirty-one, Hitler supplied a memoir of his early life to the archivist of the NSDAP, the Nazi Party: 'I was orphaned with no father or mother at seventeen and left without any financial support. My total cash at the time of the trip to Vienna was about 80 kronen. I was therefore forced immediately to earn my bread as a common labourer. I went, as a not yet eighteen-year-old, as a worker's helper on construction jobs, and had in the course of two years experienced almost all types of work of the common daily wage earner . . . After indescribable effort I succeeded to educate myself so well as a painter that I, through this activity from my twentieth year on, was able to make out in this work even if at first scantily. I became an architectural draughtsman and architectural painter and was practically completely independent by my twenty-first year. In 1912 I went in this capacity to Munich.'

This was Hitler's somewhat romanticized version. It is known that to earn money the young Hitler shovelled snow from the pavement in front of the Vienna Opera House, and that he tried for a porter's job in Vienna's Westbahnhof railway station. While he painted prolifically, including landscapes with houses and churches, he was, however, certainly not a qualified architectural draughtsman.

In the period 1907–9 he spent money on opera tickets, kid gloves and ivory-handled canes. In 1908 his aunt Johanna loaned him 924 kronen, and after his mother's death in December 1907 he received a further 652 kronen; he also received 25 kronen a month of his orphan's pension. Therefore his *unearned* income was about 80 kronen a month – equivalent to a young school-teacher's salary. So his genuinely abject poverty in the winter of 1909–10 can only be put down to very poor budgeting.

Down and Out in Vienna

REINHOLD HANISCH was a tramp who became Hitler's only friend in the charity ward at Meidling, a Vienna suburb. Hanisch was later to recall Hitler as a young man wearing a frock coat; from under a greasy black derby hat, his hair hung over his coat collar while a thick ruff of fluffy beard encircled his chin. He would hang around night shelters, living on the bread and soup he got there and discussing politics, often getting into heated arguments.

Hanisch was registered, under the false name of Fritz Walter, at a hostel for young men in Meidling, a Vienna suburb. This hostel harboured not only blue- and white-collar workers, and some craftsmen, but the flotsam of society: gamblers, money lenders, beggars, bankrupt businessmen and discharged army officers. Hanisch persuaded Hitler to move in, and he also persuaded the apathetic young painter actually to do some work.

'A Pleasure with Teddy Powder'

HITLER AND HANISCH went into partnership together on a fifty-fifty basis. Hitler copied postcards and lithographs of Viennese scenes, producing sketches and watercolours – *at the rate of one per day* – that Hanisch sold in the streets and bars of Vienna for about 5 kronen each. Hitler also produced a poster advertising a hair tonic, another for a mattress-feathers shop and another for an anti-perspirant powder sold under the brand name 'Teddy'. Yet another was for a toilet soap, and depicted a mountain of soap bars in front of the majestic St Stephan's

Cathedral. Even if the pair of near down-and-outs could not clothe themselves properly they were no longer cold and hungry.

In due course the untalented artist fell out with Hanisch over a Hellenic masterpiece on German soil, a painting of the Vienna Parliament building. Hitler thought it was worth 50 kronen, Hanisch sold it for 12; a fracas ensued, during which Hanisch was arrested and found to have no papers and to be living under a false name. Hitler instituted legal proceedings against him and at the trial on 11 August 1910, Hanisch was sentenced to seven days in jail.

In the meantime, Hitler – whose circle of friends, or at least acquaintances, included a number of Jews – continued to sell his paintings through a Hungarian art dealer called Josef Neumann, who, moreover, introduced him to three other dealers.

Hitler the Painter (1)

AFTER HANISCH HAD LEFT the men's hostel Hitler soon made friends with Josef Greiner. They shared interests in painting, music and the occult. Hitler's painting technique now improved without any formal art training. He had some natural ability and was fluent in pencil and charcoal studies, skilful as a landscape watercolourist, and indeed in oils. It was his network of Jewish art dealers who bought most of his work. When he moved from Vienna to Munich, he stayed with the Popp family (see below) and continued to paint, but sales were less successful – no Jewish art dealers. He continued to draw and paint throughout his time in the army during the Great War until his paints and artwork were stolen.

'Stateless Person'

THE MÄNNERHEIM (men's home) on Meldmanstrasse in a northern suburb of Vienna was Hitler's abode from February

1910 to May 1913. His monthly rental in the respectable hostel for men was 12 kronen. His output of paintings was sold to Josef Neumann, Samuel Morgenstern, a frame maker, Jacob Alternberg and other worthy Jewish dealers. An eyewitness at the hostel described Hitler as 'wearing a knee-length "bicycle coat" of indeterminate colour, an old, grey, soft hat with the ribbon missing, hair down to his shoulders and an unruly beard. He owned no shirt, his coat was worn through at the elbows, the soles of his shoes were patched with paper.' On his twenty-fourth birthday, 20 April 1913, Hitler became eligible to receive his outstanding share of his father's inheritance. With this sum of 820 kronen he left Vienna for Munich, where he registered as a 'stateless person', describing himself as a writer.

Chez Mr Popp, the Tailor

HITLER ARRIVED IN MUNICH on 26 May 1913, with his father's legacy to fund him. He rented a room from Mr Josef Popp, a tailor on the Schleissheimerstrasse, in the Swabing artists' quarter, for only 20 marks a month. As kind Mr Popp, a rather smart couturier, subsidized his clothing, while Hitler continued to paint – selling two paintings to Herr Heilmann, a friendly local baker, for 10 to 20 marks each; a small oil painting to a Dr Schirmer, who commissioned two watercolours from him; and to a Herr Würsler, who bought an oil painting for 25 marks – life was looking up for him, and he described his fifteen months in Munich as 'the happiest and most contented time of my life'. The comfortable, mildly profitable period came to an end on the outbreak of the Great War. On 16 August 1914 Hitler joined the 1st Bavarian Infantry Regiment.

Hitler the Painter (2)

HITLER CONTINUED TO DRAW and make architectural sketches, using red and blue pencil, until the mid-1930s. By then, of course, he was no longer selling his paintings, but, rather, bestowing them. In his memoirs Albert Speer, Hitler's favourite architect, noted:

> With a few shy words [he] gave me one of the watercolours he had done in his youth. A Gothic church done in 1909, it is executed in an extremely precise, patient and pedantic style. No personal impulses can be felt in it; not a stroke has any verve. But it is not only the brush strokes that lack all character; by its choice of subject, the flat colours, the conventional perspective, the picture seems a candid witness to this early period of Hitler. All his watercolours from the same time have this quality and even the watercolours done while he was an orderly in the First World War lack distinctiveness . . . Nevertheless he still thought well enough of the modest watercolours of his youth to give them away occasionally as a special distinction.

Speer had very high standards and was the only cultured man amongst Hitler's coterie, so his assessment of his Führer's daubs is unsurprisingly rather damning.

Hitler's First Love

HITLER'S FIRST LOVE (other than his mother, who spoiled him and whom he adored), was Stefanie (or Stephanie) Isak, a tall blonde girl who lived in the same suburb of Linz as he did. Her surname indicated that she could well be Jewish, but that did not in the least bother him. The seventeen-year-old Lothario wrote a string of romantic poems to her, and – with his great friend, Gustl Kubizek – would every day stand in the street waiting for her to walk by – unfortunately, chaperoned by her mother. For her part, Stefanie was barely aware of his existence. Hitler told Gustl that he wanted to kidnap the girl and elope with her; then, because she continued to ignore him, he planned to commit suicide by jumping in the River Danube, taking her with him. Stefanie, who probably never exchanged a word with Hitler, in due course married a soldier, Lieutenant Jansten.

Wieland the Smith

AUGUST KUBIZEK, Hitler's childhood friend and a music student, influenced him greatly. They devised ambitious architectural designs and visited the opera together. Wagner's early opera *Rienzi*, about a humble medieval Roman citizen who became a city leader, inspired Hitler to write dramas based on old German sagas, as well as an opera called *Wieland the Smith*, a Wagnerian pastiche. Kubizek later recounted all their adventures together in his book *The Young Hitler I Knew*.

The Great War: 'No Leadership Qualities'

ON 5 FEBRUARY 1914, Hitler appeared before an Army Draft Board in Salzburg, where he underwent a physical examination. The verdict was: 'Unfit for military and auxiliary service; too weak. Incapable of bearing arms.' He returned to Munich, where he was photographed among the cheering crowds in the Odeonsplatz when war was declared on 1 August. 'Thus my heart, like that of a million others overflowed with proud joy.'

A petition he wrote to the King of Bavaria, volunteering to serve in a Bavarian regiment, despite being an Austrian citizen, was successful, and he joined the 16th Bavarian Reserve Infantry Regiment, commanded by Colonel List, later writing that it was 'the greatest and most unforgettable time of my earthly existence'. Private First Class Hitler was employed as a runner or messenger (*Meldeganger*) between regimental HQ and the front-line troops. In December 1914 he received the Iron Cross Second Class, in May 1918 he was awarded a regimental certificate for bravery and on 4 August 1918 the Iron Cross First Class, which was rarely given to very junior 'other ranks'. These decorations were recommended by the Jewish regimental adjutant, Hugo Gutmann, who later reported 'we could discover no leadership qualities in him'. In October 1916 he was lightly wounded at Le Barque and sent to Beelitz hospital near Berlin, where he convalesced for six months. He fought with the List regiment in Flanders, in the battles of Arras, Chemin des Dames, Montdidier-Nyons, Soissons and Reims. In March 1917 he was promoted to lance-corporal. In October 1918, south of Ypres, he was under fire from British gas shells and, temporarily blinded, was sent back to Pasewalk hospital in Pomerania, near Stettin. His two closest comrades were Ernst Schmidt and Heinrich Bachman. Rudolf Hess also served with the same regiment. Hitler was still a 'loner', but brave and conscientious.

Hitler the Poet (2)

In the trench warfare of 1915 Hitler wrote (translated):

> I often go on chilly nights
> To the Oak of Woden in the quiet woods
> Weaving a union by the use of dark powers
> The Moon shapes runic letters with its magic spell
> And all who are full of pride in daylight's hours
> Are humbled by its magic formula!
> They draw their swords of shining steel – but instead of fighting
> They freeze into solid stalagmites
> So are the false parted from the true souls

I reach into a nest of words
And hand out gifts to the good and just
And my formula brings them blessings and riches!

Foxl – Hitler's Dog

Corporal Adolf Hitler, on duty in the Great War at Fromelles, owned a dog called Foxl. 'It was crazy how fond I was of the beast. Nobody could touch me without Foxl's instantly becoming furious. Everybody in the trenches loved him. During marches he would run all around us, observing everything, not missing a thing. I used to share everything with him. In the evening he used to live beside me.'

The dog had appeared in January 1915, chasing a rat in Hitler's trench. 'With exemplary patience (he didn't understand a word of German) I gradually got him used to me.' Foxl was English, possibly a fox terrier, and had wandered across no man's land. 'I taught him everything: how to jump over obstacles; how to climb up a ladder and down again. The essential thing is that a dog should always sleep beside its master.' Foxl went through the battles of the Somme and Arras, but eventually, between Colmar and Harpsheim, he was stolen from a train by a railway employee.

The Tatterdemalion Ballet Dancers

'When we went into the line in 1916 south of Bapaume the heat was intolerable. As we marched through the streets there was not a house, not a tree to be seen: everything had been destroyed and even the grass was burnt. It was a veritable wilderness . . . The soldier has a boundless affection for the ground on which he has shed his blood. Marching along the roads was a misery for us poor old infantrymen; again and again we were driven off the

'READ US THE FUNNY BITS'

road by the bloody gunners and again and again we had to dive into the swamps to save our skins.' Towards the end of the war Hitler and his comrades had to cut up their greatcoats to make puttees. 'We looked like a bunch of tatterdemalion ballet dancers!'

Hitler the Communist

SHORTLY AFTER THE ARMISTICE on 21 November 1918 that ended the Great War, Corporal Hitler left hospital and returned to Munich. The barracks to which he returned were run by soldiers' councils. The Soviet Republic of Bavaria, a revolutionary blend of Social Democrats and the radical Independent Social Democrats, was headed by Kurt Eisner (1867–1919). A Munich theatre critic, this Jewish Marxist journalist and very left-wing Socialist appealed to Hitler as he flirted with Communism.

As a member of the 7th Company, 1st Reserve Battalion of the Bavarian 2nd Infantry Regiment, Hitler was made *Vertrauens-mann* or representative. His duties included co-operation with the propaganda department of the revolutionary Independent Social Democratic Party of Germany. On 13 April the Communist *Räterepublik* had been proclaimed and the Munich soldiers' councils held elections to ensure that the Munich garrison stood loyally behind the 'Red Republic'. As Deputy Battalion Representative, Corporal Hitler was a supporter of a Communist 'republic', and many of his friends – 'Sepp' Dietrich, Julius Schreck, Herman Esser, Gottfried Feder and Balthaser Brandmayer – also supported the establishment of a republic. On 3 May 1919 the 'Red Army' was savagely destroyed and Munich 'liberated' with a death tally of 606 by the 'White Army' of Prussian and Württemberg troops. Nevertheless, for a brief period Hitler was a Communist.

Hitler's First Conspiracy

IN MARCH 1920 various Freikorps – private armies comprised of ex-soldiers – marched on Berlin to protest against the government's acceptance of the Versailles Treaty. A right-wing journalist, Wolfgang Kapp, was proclaimed Chancellor, and the Freikorps warriors announced the end of the liberal Weimar government. Hitler wanted a higher profile for the German Workers' Party and with his poet friend Dietrich Eckart (1868–1923) visited Berlin to join in the Kapp putsch. On arrival they found a general workers' strike protesting against Kapp, who panicked and fled. In Berlin the two would-be conspirators met General Ludendorff and Gustav von Kahr, the Bavarian leader. Hitler made the first of his many speeches to the 'Gymnastics and Sports Division', which later became the more colourful SA (*Sturmabteilung*) under Captain Ernst Röhm. Of course there was pandemonium and brawling, Hitler was arrested for a breach of the peace and was imprisoned for five weeks. His first public address after being released was a violent attack on the Jews, on the Communists, on the Social Democrats and on the financial markets. The very dangerous rabble-rouser was on his way.

The 'Machine-Gun King'

HITLER FIRST MET ERNST RÖHM (1887–1934), a tough, brutal, much-decorated war hero, in 1920. Röhm had founded the secret Iron Fist Society for radical right-wing servicemen, which Hitler joined. Then Röhm persuaded Hitler to investigate and infiltrate the German Workers' Party (DAP). Impressed by Hitler's raw intensity Röhm joined the DAP (as it was then) as member number 623. He helped fund Hitler and introduced him to influential officers and politicians in the early 1920s. Röhm's nickname was 'the machine-gun king' as he had 'acquired' quantities of weapons from various paramilitary groups. Short, overweight, scarred, with flushed cheeks, this swaggering, bellicose regular officer became Hitler's firm friend (although Röhm was homosexual) and they addressed each other familiarly as 'du'. In December 1920 Röhm and Dietrich Eckart persuaded General Ritter von Epp (1866–1947) to raise 60,000 marks from the army's secret funds to buy control of the Thule Society's newspaper, *Völkischer Beobachter* (the *People's Observer*), as a mouthpiece for the DAP. (Founded during the war for the study of old Germanic literature, the Thule Society was devoted to extreme mysticism, the occult and nationalism. The swastika was one of the society's mystic symbols. Nazi members of the Thule Society included Eckart, Drexler, Frank Rosenberg and Hess.) Hitler and Röhm remained close friends in the stormy years of struggle, 1921–23, and in 1931 Röhm became head of the SA, which by 1934 boasted 4,500,000 members.

The German Workers' Party

ANTON DREXLER, a Bavarian idealist, in 1919 set up a committee of independent workers, with an anti-foreigner and anti-Semitic policy. This was the German Workers' Party. Hitler joined it on 12 September as the seventh member of the committee. He, Drexler and Gottfried Feder (1883–1941) drew up a 25-point programme, which the committee adopted on 1 April 1920. Point 1 required the union of all Germans in a Greater Germany, Point 2 demanded the abrogation of the Versailles Treaty, while Point 4 required that Jews should be denied political or social office and those who had entered the Reich after August 1914 should be expelled.

This was the first major step in Hitler's career; in 1921 he assumed leadership of the party and Drexler was completely bypassed. Under Hitler's control the party became the NSDAP, *Nationalsozialistische Deutsche Arbeiterpartei* (National Socialist German Workers' Party), or more simply the Nazi Party. It was the first important stage in Hitler's transformation from an unemployed ex-soldier into a nascent political firebrand. It was also the terrible moment in his life when the anti-Semitism virus took hold of him and never left him. (The myth that during his hospital convalescence in 1919, Hitler had visions of 'Jewish-Bolshevik' conspiracies is, of course, nonsense.)

Sturmabteilung (SA)

THE SO-CALLED GYMNASTICS and Sports Division, a paramilitary organization founded ostensibly to keep order, was recruited from ex-service and ex-Freikorps men and initially was under the command of Ernst Röhm. To begin with, they were used to provoke trouble and disrupt other parties' meetings, particularly those of the Communists. Emil Maurice (Hitler's valet) and Johann Klintzsch were key members. On 5 October 1921 it became officially the *Sturmabteilung* (SA or 'Storm Section' of the National Socialist Movement). In 1921 and 1922 Hitler sent the SA into action in Munich and Coburg.

For Hitler the SA had primarily a political function, to be an instrument of political intimidation, but with brutal, independent *condottieri* such as Röhm, Heines and Joachim von Heydebreck among its number, it was difficult to control.

Two key officers in the SA as it grew rapidly were Rudolf Hess, who had served with Hitler in the war, and Hermann Göring, the swaggering, boisterous, but courageous ex-member of the Richthofen Fighter Squadron, of whom Hitler wrote: 'I liked him [Göring]. I made him the head of my SA. He's the only one of its heads who ran the SA properly. I gave him a dishevelled rabble. In a very short time he had organized a division of eleven thousand men.'

The Piano Player's Wife (1)

DIETRICH ECKART, poet, occultist and close friend, was responsible for Hitler's entrée into Bavarian society. He also advised Hitler to remain a bachelor in order to attract women's support for the Nazi Party. Hélène Bechstein, who was married to the famous piano manufacturer of that surname, introduced Hitler to many society women.

Hitler also met Ernst ('Putzi') Hanfstängl (1887–1976), who became his 'piano player'. A Harvard-educated son of rich art dealers from Munich, Putzi was rather a clown – tall, eccentric, incoherent and highly strung, he was popular with foreign journalists. Putzi's wife was a strikingly beautiful American, a tall, most attractive brunette – and another Hélène. In Putzi's book *Hitler: the Missing Years*, Hélène Hanfstängl admitted that Hitler was attracted to her but she did not reciprocate and thought that he had no interest in sex at all. Nevertheless Hitler plucked up courage and, to her surprise, asked Hélène, a married woman, to share her life with him. She declined and told him he ought to get married. Dolefully he explained that marriage was not an option for him: he was dedicated to his country. Hitler remained good friends with the piano player and his wife for some years more.

To Be Fit for Society

FRAU HÉLÈNE BECHSTEIN and Frau Elsa Bruckmann, another wealthy Munich hostess, competed to teach the naive and gauche Adolf Hitler the art of *salonfähig*, to be fit for polite society. They replaced his cheap blue serge suit with tailored suits, well-cut dinner jackets, smarter hats and handmade leather shoes at their expense. And they taught him the various grades of hand-kissing (five, apparently, in 1920s Munich), how to bone a trout, eat an artichoke and deal with a lobster. Of course, Hitler wanted their patronage and financial contributions to party funds, and to persuade them to join the NSDAP.

Sieg Heil and the *Hitler Song Book*

PUTZI HANFSTÄNGL dropped into Hitler's modest flat, caught sight of a beat-up old piano in the hallway and casually played a Bach prelude. Hitler then asked him if he knew any Wagner. So Putzi played extracts from *Die Meistersinger von Nürnberg*, to Hitler's amazement and excitement, and he said, 'You must play for me often. There is nothing like that to get me into tune before I have to face the public.' After that Putzi, who was a good pianist with a wide-ranging repertoire, would often play for two hours at a stretch. He recalled, 'I must have played from *Tristan and Isolde* hundreds of times and he couldn't have enough of it. It did him good physically. The music brought Hitler the relaxation he sought.' In 1924 Putzi published a *Hitler Song Book* which included titles like 'Hitler Lied' ('Hitler Song'), 'Deutsche Voran' ('Germans First') and 'Die Hitler-Medizin' ('Hitler Medicine'). Putzi knew how to compose catchy tunes and songs which went down well at Nazi Party rallies – he was, indeed, Hitler's court musician. It was Putzi's time at Harvard University, he said, that led him to make the suggestion that the Nazis should use American college-style music at political rallies to excite the crowds, in contrast to the drab respectability of the other parties. In November 1922, shortly after meeting Hitler, Putzi claimed that the chant of 'Sieg Heil' and the accompanying arm movement that became a feature of Nazi rallies was a direct copy of the technique used by American football cheerleaders, which he had taught Hitler.

Amann and the Profitable Eher Verlag

HITLER BEFRIENDED some of his comrades from the four years of frontline soldiering with the 1st Bavarian Infantry Regiment. Not the Jewish Leutnant Hugo Gutmann, who recommended Hitler for the Iron Cross First Class, but Leutnant Fritz Wiedemann, who became his adjutant in 1935–9, and most certainly with tough Max Amann (1891–1957), his sergeant, who became his literary agent, his publisher and his financial advisor. On 17 December 1920 control of Eher Verlag, the publisher of the *Völkischer Beobachter*, a rather rundown newspaper that was printed twice a week with a circulation of 7,000, passed to Anton Drexler, the nominal president of the *Deutsche Arbeiterpartei* (DAP). In the next few years Hitler and Amann, with help from the printer Adolf Müller, a Nazi supporter, and a 'loan' of a thousand dollars from Hanfstängl, turned the paper round to become a daily in the 'American' format of 21 inches by 18 inches, with 16 pages; by 1923, its circulation was between 20,000 and 30,000 copies. Hitler gave every appearance of being its new owner and it became *the* Nazi newspaper. Under Amann's shrewd management the paper cleared all its debts and became highly profitable. By 1933 it was still a Munich paper and had a circulation of 127,000. That year saw editions printed simultaneously in Berlin and Vienna. By 1941 it had reached 1,200,000, and received huge advertising revenues. Amann and Hitler earned immense sums and the former channelled Hitler's share into Switzerland and the Netherlands.

Hitler's Photographer and Court Jester

HEINRICH HOFFMANN (1885–1957) was the son of a successful photographer and learned his craft in his father's business. In the Great War he served as a photographer in the Bavarian Army and published his first book of photographs in 1919, from which he made a lot of money; two years later he became Hitler's personal photographer. Hoffman, and his family in Munich, introduced Hitler to society and encouraged him in his art collecting. Through Hoffman, Hitler also met Dr Theodor Morell (1890–1948), who for nine years treated him with various cranky 'cures', and Eva Braun, who worked in Hoffman's studio.

'I know three people who when they're together, never stop laughing. They're Hoffmann, Amann and Goebbels . . . I'm very fond of Hoffman. He's a man who always makes fun of me. He's a "dead-pan" humorist and he never fails to find a victim,' Hitler declared to his merry dinner companions in February 1942. The former Nazi newspaperman Kurt Lüdecke, writing in 1938 after he'd fled Germany, noted, 'Hoffman was an ideal companion, humorous and amusing, a good story-teller with plenty of what the Germans call "mother-wit". At Haus Wachenfeld, Kannenberg with his accordion and Hoffmann are said to be a team that can make Hitler laugh himself sick. I found plenty of horse-sense behind his jester's mask and we had a rollicking time.'

Hoffmann was elected to the Reichstag in 1933, was made a professor and earned a fortune from the sales of a series of excellent photographs. He also published a book of photographs taken by Eva Braun and her sister.

The Air Ace

HERMANN GÖRING (1893–1946) was born in Rosenheim, Bavaria to minor gentry. He fought in the Great War, initially in the infantry and then as a brilliant fighter pilot. He became a hero, gained twenty-two victories, earned the 'Pour le Mérite' medal and commanded the famous Richthofen squadron. After the war he flew a Fokker monoplane at air displays and as a dashing twenty-six-year-old lieutenant met his first wife, Karin, who was five years older than him. He attended Munich University to study political science and history. At a mass demonstration in Königsplatz in November 1922 he first met Hitler – intense, pale, with his small moustache, slouch hat and carrying a dog whip. Soon, at the Monday evening 'court' at the Café Neumaier, Göring and Karin were listening to Hitler at his regular table. One phrase struck Göring forcibly – it was useless, Hitler said, to make empty threats and protests about the Versailles Peace Treaty and the extradition of the German Army commanders: 'You've got to have bayonets to back up threats.' The next day Göring, after consultation with Karin, offered his services to Hitler, who was delighted. 'Splendid, a war ace with the "Pour le Mérite" – imagine it! Excellent propaganda! Moreover he has money and doesn't cost me a cent.' He said all this to his close supporter Kurt Lüdecke. In return Hitler 'promised' Göring he would become leader of the Reich.

The Dishevelled Rabble

GÖRING AND HIS WIFE bought a villa with elegant furnishings in Obermenzing, a fashionable suburb of Munich, mainly with her money. Hitler became a frequent guest, arriving late at night and listening to Göring singing ballads, operatic arias and folk songs in a reasonable baritone. Hitler's group in 1923 reserved a large table, their *Stammtisch,* in the Bratwurstglöckel Tavern in the heart of old Munich. At the Easter rally for the SA Hitler used Göring's beautiful 25-horsepower Mercedes-Benz 16 as a saluting base and at the same rally Göring was reportedly seen giving Hitler pocket money! However, their relationship was never intimate – always 'sie', never 'du'.

At that time the SA was an ill-organized club of ex-Freikorps, street brawlers and roughs, who used as weapons brass knuckle-dusters, rubber truncheons, chair legs, beer steins, occasionally pistols and home-made bombs. Germany was in a terrible state. There were about fifty organizations, almost parties, of Great War veterans, often fighting each other. At the beginning of 1923 the mark was valued at 7,000 to the US dollar. By the end of the year it had reached a million, then billions and finally trillions of marks to the dollar. The government refused to stop the printing presses and balance the national budget. It was an ideal time for Hitler, and his first Reich Party rally took place with 6,000 'stormtroopers' in Munich in January 1923.

Du

IN GERMANY close friends are addressed as 'du' (the equivalent of the French 'tu'). Albert Speer, a dedicated Hitler-watcher, and Rudolf Hess, a friend of Hitler's, agreed that there were only five people who could call Hitler 'du':

Dietrich Eckart, a nationalist poet (1868–1923) and an early friend of Hitler's, whose 'Storm Song' ('Germany awake! Break your chains') was a favourite marching song. He was an alcoholic and when he died aged fifty-five, Hitler recalled: 'He shone in our eyes like the polar star.'

Herman Esser, State Secretary for Tourism (1900–81), was a co-founder of the German Workers' Party, a young ex-soldier, an orator and a gutter journalist who wrote for the *Völkisher Beobachter*. He was also a Jew-baiter and a lecherous, crude, noisy thug. An early worshipper, he was the first to call Hitler 'Führer' in public. In 1933, however, Esser was demoted to the formal 'sie'.

Christian Weber, a former horse-dealer, who brandished a dog whip and brawled with Communists, was foolhardy enough to mock *Mein Kampf* to its author. Thereafter Hitler avoided him.

Julius Streicher, a shaven-headed, Jew-hating war veteran, and Ernst Röhm were the remaining 'close friends', but in fact Hitler treated Streicher impersonally and later demoted him to 'sie', while Röhm was murdered on Hitler's orders.

'Hitler is Germany: Germany is Hitler'

RUDOLF HESS (1894–1987) served in the same Bavarian regiment as Hitler in the Great War, a brave, disciplined and intensely patriotic young officer. Wounded in 1917 he transferred to the Imperial German Military Air Service and after the war joined the Thule Society. In 1919 Hess joined Epp's Freikorps and proved to be a reckless, brutal street fighter. In May 1920 he heard Hitler speak at a DAP meeting in Munich and returned home to tell his future wife, Ilse Pröhl, 'A man – I've heard a man: he's unknown, I've forgotten his name. But if anyone can free us from Versailles, then it's this man. This unknown man will restore our honour!' As a member of the new National Socialist German Workers' Party Hess was soon to become a close associate of Hitler, and in 1921 he formed a 100-strong SA troop among Munich fellow students. Before long he was Hitler's most intimate and trusted confidant, earning the nicknames 'Fraülein Hess' or 'Frau Hitler' (though fiercely heterosexual), and guarding Hitler's interests with a ferocious jealousy. The perfect backroom boy, he controlled the organization of the NSDAP, revelling in the Nazi uniforms, parades and bands. He too could deliver powerful rabble-rousing speeches. By 1932 he was an SS Obergruppenführer and Chairman of the Central Political Commission of the Nazi Party, and Hitler named him to follow Göring in the leadership succession. A tall, dark-browed, intensely proud man, he burned with a religious fervour for his leader and believed that 'Hitler is Germany: Germany is Hitler.'

The 'Unpadded Skeleton' and Leather Shorts

FRIEDELIND WAGNER, the composer's granddaughter, recalled the young Hitler 'in Bavarian leather breeches, short, thick woollen socks, a red-blue-checked shirt and a short blue jacket that bagged about his unpadded skeleton. His sharp cheekbones stuck out over hollow, pasty cheeks and above them was a pair of unnaturally bright-blue eyes. There was a half-starved look about him, but something else too, a sort of fanatical look.' He did own a decent blue suit and, rather surprisingly, a dinner jacket and tails in which to go to the opera. Before he became famous he was much attached to Bavarian-style leather short trousers. 'The healthiest clothing, without any doubt, is leather shorts, shoes and stockings. Having to change into long trousers was always a misery to me. Even with a temperature of ten below zero I used to go about in leather shorts. The feeling of freedom they give you is wonderful. Abandoning my shorts was one of the biggest sacrifices I had to make. I only did it for the sake of North Germany . . . Quite a number of the young people of today [August 1942] wear shorts all the year around . . . In the future I shall have an SS Highland Brigade in leather shorts!'

Nevertheless, after Hitler became Chancellor in 1933 he was rarely, if ever, photographed in leather shorts – not *comme il faut* for a Führer.

The Piano Player's Wife (2)

HÉLÈNE HANFSTÄNGL recalled how she first met Hitler, in 1922: 'He was at the time a slim, shy young man with a faraway look in his very blue eyes. He was dressed almost shabbily – a cheap white shirt, black tie, a worn dark blue suit, with which he wore an incongruous dark brown leather vest, a beige-coloured trench coat, much the worse for wear, cheap black shoes and a soft, old greyish hat. His appearance was quite pathetic.' Hitler was besotted with her. He once went down on his knees to her to proclaim his love, and for many years he sent her flowers on her birthday. He was kind to young Egon, her son, and after he became Chancellor in 1933 invited them both to stay at Haus Wachenfeld, before it became the Berghof. Egon, then twelve, admired Hitler's collection of sixty-four Wild West novels by Karl May. Hitler talked to Egon about motorcars, engines, the size and performance of various ships, and technical things of interest to a young boy. When Hélène eventually divorced Putzi in 1936, Hitler was said to be pleased – Putzi had by then fallen out of favour with him. She escaped from Germany in 1938 and returned to her native America.

The Moustache Dialogue

THE LITTLE BLACK MOUSTACHES of Adolf Hitler and Charlie Chaplin must have been the most famous in the world in the mid-twentieth century. In the Munich and Bavarian dialect that type of moustache was called a *Rotzbremse* or 'snot brake'! Putzi Hanfstängl told Hitler shortly after meeting him that he should grow his moustache right across his mouth, 'Look at the portraits by Holbein and Van Dyck; the old masters would never have dreamt of such an ugly fashion.' To which Hitler answered, 'Don't worry about my moustache. If it is not the fashion now, it will be later because I wear it.' And so it turned out.

The Munich Beer Cellar Putsch Stage 1

INSPIRED BY Mussolini's successful 'march on Rome' in 1922 – his takeover of the Italian state – the thirty-four-year-old Hitler decided in the autumn of 1923 that with rocketing inflation the German economy was on the verge of collapse. A successful putsch seizing control of Bavaria with a powerful force mainly of SA under Hermann Göring and Ernest Röhm's *Reichskriegsflagge* (the paramilitary wing of the Nazi Party) starting in Munich might destroy the Bavarian government. On Thursday, 8 November a fanatical Hitler in a long, black overcoat headed a motley rabble of armed SA men who burst into Munich's Bürgerbräukeller. He leapt onto a chair, fired his pistol upwards and shouted, 'A national revolution in Munich has just broken out. The whole city is at this moment occupied by our troops. The hall is surrounded by 600 men.' This was, of course, quite untrue.

Röhm's men had at the same time surrounded the War Ministry. Heinrich Himmler as Röhm's flag-bearer posed dramatically for the press photographers. Hitler took Gustav von Kahr, the Bavarian State Commissioner, General Otto von Lossow, commander of the Bavarian Army, and Colonel Hans von Seisser, head of the Bavarian State Police, as prisoners and then promised them top jobs in his 'new' Germany under General Erich Ludendorff. He made a notable speech to the beer cellar's political crowd, then waited for Ludendorff to arrive. Ludendorff was somewhat taken aback but allowed himself to be persuaded by Hitler that this was the way to go, and at Hitler's behest then persuaded Kahr, von Lossow and Seisser to agree to join the putsch. So far so good!

The Munich Beer Cellar Putsch Stage 2

THE KEY TO MOST political putsches is to secure control of the communications system. Hitler, Göring and Röhm were of course amateurs – and they failed to control the telephone exchange and lines. That was the first major mistake. The second mistake was to trust Kahr and Lossow, who broke their promise to join the plotters. That night Ludendorff allowed them to leave; Hitler was dumbfounded to find his key hostages had disappeared. The next day there was a pitched battle. Hitler, Ludendorff, Röhm and Göring led 2,000 followers into the Odeonsplatz in the centre of Munich where state police and soldiers confronted them. It was a battle – a fracas perhaps – in which three police and fourteen Nazis were killed. Göring was wounded and Hitler dislocated his shoulder when he tripped over. General Ludendorff hit the ground at the first volley, was promptly arrested and then claimed he was an innocent bystander. Hitler was given shelter for a few days by his friends the Hanfstängls, during which he apparently put a gun to his head and had to be restrained by the beautiful Hélène Hanfstängl from committing suicide.

The London *Times* correspondent reporting the putsch described Hitler as 'a little man . . . unshaven with disorderly hair and so hoarse that he could hardly speak.'

In spite of its failure the pathetic Munich Beer Cellar putsch became part of Nazi mythology.

Trial for Treason

FOR TWENTY-FOUR DAYS from 26 February 1924, Hitler and those of his cohorts who had not been killed or escaped stood trial in a courtroom in the Infantry School in the Blutenburgstrasse, Munich, accused of high treason. Among them were General Ludendorff, Rudolf Hess, Wilhelm Frick, Hermann Kriebel, Emil Maurice and Ernst Röhm. Otto von Lossow was among those who testified against Hitler. The trial was front-page news in every German newspaper, as Hitler took full responsibility for leading the SA stormtroopers and the rest of the *Kampfbund* (Hitler's 'Battle League') in the ill-fated putsch. He dominated the court. 'It is not you gentlemen who pass judgement on us. That judgement is spoken by the eternal court of history . . . That court will not ask us "Did you commit

'LET THE GERMAN PEOPLE DECIDE!'

high treason, or did you not?" That court will judge us . . . as Germans who wanted only the good of their own people and Fatherland; who wanted to fight and die . . . You may pronounce us guilty a thousand times over . . .'

The judges were sympathetic; he had the right idea, in their view, even if his actions were misguided. Ludendorff, hero of the Great War, was acquitted, and Hitler was given the minimum sentence of five years' imprisonment. He was released after serving nine months in jail – and immediately resumed his political activities.

School of Higher Education

WHEN HITLER ARRIVED in the Landsberg prison, nursing his dislocated shoulder, he was so dispirited that he went on hunger strike. Anton Drexler, Hélène Hanfstängl and Hélène Bechstein together persuaded him to return to a normal life. Hitler's party had been declared illegal and his stormtroopers and some of the other leaders went underground.

Landsberg prison, fifty miles west of Munich, was reasonably comfortable and Hitler and his fellow-Nazi prisoners had a relaxed life, with good food, a garden and as many newspapers and books as they wished. Hitler read voraciously – Nietzsche, Marx, Treitschke, Bismarck, and various political, racist and occult works – and the prison became his 'school of higher education'.

He received favoured treatment and had as many visitors as he liked in cell No.7 on the first floor, which he shared with Rudolf Hess, Friedrich Weber and Colonel Hermann Kriebel. The other prisoners and all the guards fell under his spell, and he enjoyed holding court to them. The dining room where he presided was decorated with a huge Nazi swastika banner. His thirty-fifth birthday, on 20 April, found his cell swamped with flowers and gifts. While there, Hitler dictated *Mein Kampf*, initially to his chauffeur, Emil Maurice, and then to Rudolf Hess, who joined him voluntarily as a prisoner.

Lebensraum **and Geopolitics**

IN LANDSBERG PRISON Hess introduced Hitler to Karl Haushofer (1869–1946), the Professor of Political Geography at Munich University, for whom Hess had worked as scientific assistant. Haushofer visited them at the prison and spent hours talking to Hitler, assisting with and perhaps influencing *Mein Kampf*, particularly where Hitler was writing about occult training, political affairs and *Lebensraum* ('living space'). Haushofer, a retired general, believed that a nation's ability to grow and prosper depended largely on living space. He was also the exponent of the idea and theory of geopolitics, which saw the oceanic power of the British Empire being superseded by Germany's continental power. Nevertheless, he believed in the *complementary* nature of German and British power. Hitler came out of Landsberg with two key ideas, which dominated most of the rest of his life: that *Lebensraum* was essential for Nazi Germany; and that Germany and England should live and work together, one on land, the other on the high seas.

Hitler's 'Business Dwarf'

KURT LÜDECKE knew Max Amann, the Nazi Party's business manager, and described him in 1932 as a 'little man, strong and active looking, with a heavy head on a short neck, almost lost between his shoulders. I was aware again of his prominent nose and small, peculiarly brilliant blue eyes . . .' Amann was born in Munich on 24 November 1891 and died there in extreme poverty twelve years after the Second World War. From 1915 to

1918 he was Hitler's company sergeant, and joined the SA in 1921. His business training meant that he became Party treasurer and manager of the Party newspaper, the *Völkischer Beobachter*. From 1925 onwards he became essential to Hitler, arranged publication of *Mein Kampf* and skilfully banked or invested the considerable royalties, some in Munich but also in Switzerland and Holland. Amann had several illegitimate children and his wife tried unsuccessfully to drown herself. On the evening of 22 February 1942 Hitler told Himmler, 'Amann is one of the oldest of my companions. He was infinitely valuable to me for I had no notion of what double-entry book-keeping was . . . I can say positively that he's a genius. He's the greatest newspaper proprietor in the world . . . Rothermere and Beaverbrook are mere dwarfs compared to him.' Very intelligently, Amann created on the side the Hoheneichen Publishing Co. whose name covered certain publications. He behaved as if the editorial staff and the editors were nothing but a necessary evil. But he earned his Führer a small fortune.

Mein Kampf 'Lies, Stupidity and Cowardice'

FROM JULY 1924 Hitler started to dictate *Mein Kampf*, taken down by Hess and Emil Maurice. After leaving prison – his war record counted in his favour and the Bavarian Supreme Court released him on 19 December 1924 – he went to the town of Berchtesgaden to finish his book: 'I lived there like a fighting cock. I was very fond of visiting the Dreimäderl Haus where there were always pretty girls.'

As well as being the business manager of the Nazi Party, Max Amann was director of the Nazi publishing house Eher Verlag, which eventually published *Mein Kampf*. Hitler's own title had been *Four and a Half Years of Struggle Against Lies, Stupidity and Cowardice*. Amann hoped for a dramatic and sensational content, and changed the title of the extremely long, boring, turgid, rambling book to *Mein Kampf* (*My Struggle*). Additional input and editing to Hitler's book came from Müller, the printer, Putzi Hanfstängl, Josef Stolzing-Czerny, music critic of the *Völkisher Beobachter*, and Bernard Stempfle, once editor of the Bavarian newspaper *Miesbacher Anzeiger*. All the elements of National Socialist ideology are contained in the book: nationalism, anti-Bolshevism, anti-Semitism, the purity of the Aryan race and *Lebensraum* – the need for more space, to be obtained by a continental war of conquest. There was a clear warning to the world from the thirty-five-year-old prisoner, who had considerable influence in Germany but as yet no power. The first volume was published in summer 1925; it was 400 pages long and cost 12 Reichsmarks. The second volume appeared in 1926. By 1940 6 million copies had been sold. The edition published in the USA was called *My Battle*; in Italy it was entitled *La Mia Battaglia* and in Spain *Mi Lucha*. Royalties from *Mein Kampf* kept Hitler solvent – from 1925 to 1929 these averaged 15,000 Reichsmarks annually. For all that it sold so many copies, however, the world largely remained inattentive.

Hitler's Secret Bank Account

BETWEEN 1921 AND 1922 and certainly in 1923 Hitler visited Switzerland. On 5 August 1943 he told his dinner companions, 'In 1923 I was in Switzerland, and I remember a meal in Zurich at which the number of courses completely flabbergasted me.' He was there with either Max Amann or Dr Emil Gansser, to raise funds in support of his NSDAP, and was reported to have returned from one trip to Zurich with a steamer trunk stuffed with Swiss francs and American dollars. (*The Jewish Chronicle* of 6 September 1996 disclosed that Hitler's bank account was in Bern with the Union Bank of Switzerland.) The putsch, however, lost Hitler and the NSDAP much if not all of this financial support, so the NSDAP finances were depleted, until in 1925 a certain Franz Xaver Schwarz, a treasurer of the Munich city council and member of the NSDAP, volunteered his services, took over some of Amann's duties and started to work wonders on the party's funds. He held the position of National Treasurer until the end of the Third Reich in 1945.

Hitler's 'Tough 'Uns'

IN SEPTEMBER 1927, Hitler appointed Heinrich Himmler, a brilliant organizer and a devoted follower of Hitler, who had briefly been a chicken farmer, Deputy Reichsführer of the *Schutzstaffel* (SS). Born in Landshut, Bavaria, in 1900, Himmler became perhaps, after Hitler, the most evil man in Europe. Hitler told his supper companions on 3 January 1942, 'Being convinced that there are always circumstances in which elite troops are called for, in 1922–23 I created the "Adolf Hitler Shock Troops". They were made up of men who were ready for revolution and knew that one day or another things would come to hard knocks. When I came out of Landsberg [prison], everything was broken up and scattered in sometimes rival hands. I told myself then that I needed a bodyguard, even a very restricted one, but made up of men who would be enlisted without restriction, even to march against their own brothers. Only twenty men to a city (on condition that one could count on them absolutely) rather than a suspect mass. It was [Emil] Maurice, [Julius] Schreck and [Erhard] Heiden who formed in Munich the first group of "tough 'uns" and were thus the origin of the SS. But it was with Himmler that the SS became that extraordinary body of men, devoted to an idea, loyal unto death. I see in Himmler our Ignatius de Loyola. With intelligence and obstinacy, against wind and tide, he forged this instrument . . . The SS knows that its job is to set an example, to be and not to seem, and that all eyes are upon it.'

Hitler's Russian Philosopher

ALFRED ROSENBERG (1893–1946), architect and engineer, was born of German parents in Russian Estonia and fought in the Russian Army in the Great War. Opposed to Bolshevism, he left his country in 1918 after the Russian Revolution and went as a refugee to Munich, where his anti-Semitic and anti-communist leanings led him to join the Thule Society right-wing nationalistic club; he also organized the 'Fighting League for German Culture', a union for lawyers, physicians and teachers; he contributed to the *Völkischer Beobachter*, of which he became editor in 1923; he joined the National Socialist German Workers' Party (several months before Hitler); and he marched with Hitler and Ludendorff in the 1923 Beer Hall putsch, but ran like a rabbit when the shooting started. Hitler, however, obviously thought highly of him and made him Party leader whilst he, Hitler, was in prison.

In 1930 Rosenberg published *The Myth of the Twentieth Century*, which, with *Mein Kampf*, was regarded as reflecting essential Nazi thinking. Hitler's opinion was that Rosenberg, with his Russian-speaking background, was an expert on Bolshevism, but not a manager. William Shirer, the American journalist who broadcast from Berlin during the Third Reich and up to the end of the first year of the Second World War, and published several books, famously *The Rise and Fall of the Third Reich* (1960), thought that what Rosenberg 'lacked in repulsiveness, he made up in befuddlement'. The official Nazi 'philosopher' was tedious, muddled, verbose and plain stupid. In 1933 Hitler put him in charge of the Party's foreign-affairs department and then, typically, allowed Joachim von Ribbentrop to compete with his own Foreign Bureau. Many of his enemies in the Nazi Party, particularly Goebbels and Strasser, accused Rosenberg of having Jewish blood. He bought paintings and sculptures on behalf of Hitler for the Munich Art Gallery, and for Hitler's 'dream' museum planned for Linz, and from 1940 his task force helped to loot European art treasures. In 1941 Hitler made him minister for the captured eastern territories. He was quite useless, of course, but he could speak Russian!

Hitler's Tubby Printer (1)

OPPOSITE the photographic studios of Heinrich Hoffmann, Hitler's personal photographer, was the printing plant of M. Müller u. Sohn at Schellingstrasse 39, Munich. Adolf Müller, small, stout and almost stone deaf, was, to quote Hitler's friend Dietrich Eckart, who introduced Hitler to him, 'as black as the devil . . . and more cunning than the cunningest peasant, but he's the best printer I've known in my life, and also the most generous man.' Müller had been a supporter of the Nazi Party since its inception, and with help from the ubiquitous Max Amann, a shareholder of Müller's, the tubby printer secured the contract for all the Nazi Party material including books and the *Völkischer Beobachter*. In the early 1920s Müller taught Hitler how to drive. Until the November 1923 putsch, business had been good and the two Adolfs were friends; indeed, it was Müller and Amann who came to greet and collect Hitler from the Landsberg prison. In the critical time after Hitler's release from prison it was Müller who advanced cash and printed Hitler's newspaper and book on credit. By 1928 Müller was a very wealthy man with a luxurious house at St Quirin on the shores of Te Gernsee, south of Munich. Hitler and the NSDAP leaders used Müller's house for conferences, and after his niece Geli's suicide in September 1931 a distraught Hitler took refuge with Müller.

Bavarian Ladies

EMIL MAURICE, Hitler's chauffeur and for many years a good friend, visited life classes with his Führer to gaze at the naked female models posing for artists. They would visit nightclubs in Munich and even pick up girls on the streets. Hitler would sometimes bring a woman back to his room and always presented her with flowers. The sister of one of his drivers – Jenny Haug, who habitually carried a gun with her as an extra bodyguard – was in love with him. Putzi Hanfstängl wrote that Hitler had a collection of pornographic books, most of them written by Jewish authors, and Hitler was fascinated by the Berlin women boxers.

There is evidence that Hitler had an affair in 1936 with Mitzi Reiter, a sixteen-year-old girl who ran a boutique with her older sister. Before long she became his mistress; he called her Mizzerl, Mimilein, Mizzi or Mimi and she called him Wolf, but it was the same story. She wanted marriage, perhaps to him, or at least to someone she loved. Poor besotted Mitzi, jealous of Hitler's attentions elsewhere, tried to hang herself, but was saved from death by her brother-in-law. By this time Hitler was involved with his own niece.

Hitler's Sweet Tooth

ANGELA RAUBAL, Hitler's widowed half-sister, suggested to him that Haus Wachenfeld in the Obersalzberg, which he rented in October 1928, needed a resident housekeeper and that she should be his cook/housekeeper. He remembered with pleasure the rich, sugary cakes she used to make, and Hitler's photographer's daughter, Henriette Hoffmann, recalled that 'she was a kindly, sympathetic woman, an expert in cooking Austrian specialities. She could make feather-light puff pastry, plum cakes

✠ ──────────────────────────────────── ✠

with cinnamon, spongy poppyseed strudel and fragrant vanilla pancakes – all the irresistible things her brother loved eating.' Angela also had two nubile daughters, Angela (Geli) and Elfriede.

Hitler's Tubby Printer (2)

HITLER SAID that Adolf Müller's first words to him were, '"To prevent any misunderstanding from arising let it be clearly understood that, where there's no payment, there's no printing either." Müller would only accept orders for pamphlets against cash payment. He refused dubious orders by saying that his workmen fed themselves not on political convictions, but on the pay he gave them. When one visited him, Müller never ceased to groan. Nevertheless he grew fatter and fatter. He printed more and more. He constantly bought new machines but his leitmotiv was "I can't get along on these rates. I'm ruining myself" . . . His press is equipped in the most modern style. He's a real genius in the Party.'

Whenever Müller upped his printing rates Hitler would throw a tantrum, but as Müller was stone deaf it had no effect at all. Despite his girth he was a determined Lothario, with a divorced wife, several mistresses and many bastard offspring. Hitler knew that Müller was very generous and that on each new arrival he gave the mother 5,000 marks. His working week involved two days supervising his printing works, two days with his divorced wife and two days with his mistress of the moment. As Hitler said of him, 'That Müller, he's quite a fellow.'

'Onkel Alf'

THERE SEEMS NO DOUBT that Hitler was deeply in love with his niece. Geli Raubal, younger daughter of his half-sister

Angela Geli (1908–31) accompanied her mother to keep house for Hitler on the Obersalzberg in 1925. The pretty blonde girl of seventeen had her own room in the rented villa, Haus Wachenfeld, and also, a few years later, in No.16 Prinzregentenstrasse, a smart nine-roomed flat in Munich. For six years their romance prospered; possibly it was not consummated. Geli called Hitler 'Onkel Alf'. She loved the theatre and opera and took singing and acting lessons. He idolized the girl, who was flattered and impressed by her famous uncle. In the early summer of 1928 Emil Maurice, his chauffeur, by chance surprised Hitler in Geli's room. Hitler, who always carried a riding whip with him, tried to thrash Maurice, who escaped by jumping out of a window. Hitler was insanely jealous over Geli. He refused to let her have any life of her own and did not allow her to go to Vienna to have her voice trained. When he discovered that she had allowed Maurice to make love to her he was furious. On 17 September 1931 Hitler left Munich with Hoffmann, his photographer and close friend, for Hamburg. On the way, in Nuremberg, Hess telephoned to say that Geli had shot herself dead with Hitler's 6.35mm Walther pistol in Hitler's flat. For days he was inconsolable and his friends feared for his life. He refused to eat meat thereafter. According to many witnesses Geli was the only woman he ever loved. Her room at the Berghof was kept exactly as she had left it with her carnival costume, books and white furniture. Her photograph hung in his room in Munich and in Berlin and flowers were always placed before it on the anniversary of her birth and of her death. A bust of Geli was set up in her room and every year he visited her grave. Needless to say there was a great deal of discreditable rumour, and he lamented that 'terrible filth' was killing him.

Goebbels on Hitler – Disillusionment

JOSEPH GOEBBELS was among the first to join the Nazi Party when the ban was lifted from it in February 1925. When he was fired from his job on the *Völkische Freiheit* he moved to Eberfeld. From October 1924 he made 189 political speeches in the course of a year. Initially he and Hitler were at loggerheads. At one meeting he leapt to his feet screaming, 'I demand that the petty bourgeois Adolf Hitler be expelled from the Nazi Party!' and in his diary he wrote, 'I feel battered. What sort of Hitler is this? A reactionary? Extremely awkward and uncertain. Russian question completely wrong. Italy and England our natural allies. Terrible! Our task is the annihilation of Bolshevism. Bolshevism is a Jewish creation! We must be Russia's heir! 180 millions!' At the next public meeting he confessed, 'I no longer have complete faith in Hitler. That's the terrible thing. My props have been taken away from under me.'

Happy Hitler Youth

FOR YOUNG BOYS aged ten to fourteen the Nazi Party set up the *Jungvolk*, and for girls the *Jungmädel*. To enter the *Jungvolk* a boy, known as a *Pimpf*, had to pass an initiation test. He had to learn key points of Nazi dogma, recite the Horst Wessel Song, learn arms drill (with a broomstick instead of a rifle), practise semaphore, join in strenuous two-day cross-country walks and sprint 50 metres in 12 seconds. All this was in preparation to join the *Hitler Jugend* ('Hitler Youth') for the age group fourteen to eighteen. The Hitler Youth was founded in 1926 as a branch of the SA and by 1934 had a membership of 3.5 million. They had immense pride in their uniform, their military training and discipline. Their special dagger was inscribed 'Blut und Ehre' – 'Blood and Honour'. The Hitler Youth fought and died bravely in Normandy in 1944 and during the defence of Berlin in 1945. Hitler told them, 'You are destined to be warriors for Greater Germany'. One important song (translated) was:

> 'We are the Happy Hitler Youth
> We do not need the virtues of the church
> For it is our Führer Adolf Hitler
> Who stands at our side.'

Die Alte Kämpfer – the 'Old Fighters'

DURING THE *Kampfzeit*, the 'times of struggle', Hitler had shared comradeship and occasionally danger with the 'old fighters', some of them street thugs. His familiars of the Nazi old guard were Goebbels, Dr Robert Ley, Hess, Martin Bormann, Julius Streicher, Christian Weber, Max Amann (the Party treasurer), Heinrich Hoffman (the court photographer and jester), his two adjutants, Julius Schaub and Wilhelm Brückner, and one of the SA's founders, Julius Schreck. It was when in this intimate circle talking over the old days that Hitler was most at ease. From time to time Sepp Dietrich, the brutal commander of his SS guard, Otto Dietrich, Reich press chief, Gauleiter Adolf Wagner, Hermann Esser, State Secretary for Tourism, and, later on, Albert Speer would be invited to join the Hitler coterie. They talked together in the café-restaurant Osteria Bavaria, Café Heck, Carlton's Tearooms, or in Hitler's Munich flat, or away in the Obersalzberg or Berghof. It was rare to see Himmler or Göring, but occasionally Goebbels or Hess would be invited. Women were not asked, apart from the two rather outrageous Mitford girls (see later). It was important for one's prestige to attend these meals and keep abreast of Hitler's daily opinions. Speer describes a typical late lunch at the Osteria: 'On the street several hundred people would be waiting, for our presence was indication enough that *he* would be coming. Shouts of rejoicing outside. Hitler headed toward our regular corner which was shielded on one side by a low partition. In good weather we sat in the small courtyard where there was a hint of an arbour. Hitler gave the owner and the two waitresses a jovial greeting, "What's good today?"'

Hitler's Occult Advisor

IN THE LATE 1920s Hitler discovered an occult advisor, Erik Jan Hanussen, a Jewish 'clairvoyant', who earned a great deal of money in theatres. His real name was Hermann Steinschneider and he genuinely did have extraordinary predictive abilities. When he first met Hitler at a society reception in Berlin he suggested to the Nazi leader that his elocution and speech could be improved. Surprisingly, Hitler – politely – asked Hanussen for his recommendations. He was told that although his timing and delivery were impressive, he should improve his body language and gestures and that this would have a greater impact on his audience. And it did. For the next few years the Jewish clairvoyant was Hitler's 'special' guru and moreover was asked to advise Hitler on his choice of colleagues, based on his clairvoyant and astrological gifts. On 24 February 1933 Hanussen held a séance in Berlin for a number of important people. He predicted that a large Berlin building would be engulfed in flames, and the Reichstag was set on fire and more or less demolished three days later. In April 1933 by order of Count Wolf Helldorf, Chief of Police of Potsdam, Hanussen was kidnapped from outside a theatre and murdered in a wood near Berlin.

'Those Big Blue Eyes'

JOSEPH GOEBBELS noted in his diary entry for 6 November 1925, of his first meeting with Hitler: 'We drive to Hitler. He is having his meal. He jumps to his feet, there he is. Shakes my hand like an old friend. And those big blue eyes like stars. He is glad to see me. I am in heaven. That man has got everything to be a king. A born tribune. The coming dictator.' And on 23 November, 'Hitler is there. Great joy. He greets me like an old friend. And looks after me. How I love him! What a fellow. Then he speaks. How small I am! He gives me his photograph . . . Heil Hitler! I want Hitler to be my friend.' In mid-February 1926 the diary records, 'Adolf Hitler, I love you.' Hitler had this extraordinary effect. He seduced his camp followers. All this seven years before Hitler became Chancellor, and nearly twenty years before both he and Goebbels committed suicide in the Berlin bunker.

Hitler and the Wagner Family

RICHARD WAGNER had always been Hitler's favourite composer, and Winifred Wagner, who was married to the composer's son, Siegfried, became one of the women closest to Hitler. Born Winifred Williams in Hastings, Sussex, she was widowed in 1930 but continued to run the Wagner festival at Bayreuth almost single-handedly. Attending the festival each year was a high point in Hitler's life, and he nearly always stayed with Frau Wagner in Haus Wahnfried, a grandiose house built by Wagner. Hitler was introduced by the Bechsteins, the famous piano makers, to Siegfried and Winifred in the 1920s. Siegfried thought young Hitler was a fraud. Winifred thought he was 'destined to be the saviour of Germany' and always in private called him 'Uncle Wolf', his secret name when they first met.

Joseph Goebbels's Damascus

GOEBBELS WAS INVITED to join Hitler for a holiday in Berchtesgaden in July 1926, along with Hitler's secretary, Rudolf

Hess, his chauffeur Emil Maurice, his photographer Heinrich Hoffman and Gregor Strasser (1892–1934), a radical Nazi leader. Hitler was working on the second volume of *Mein Kampf*. In this intimate magic circle the twenty-eight-year-old Goebbels soon met what Strasser and his lieutenant, Karl Kaufmann, described as 'Joseph Goebbels's Damascus'. Goebbels became infatuated: 'He [Hitler] is a genius. The natural creative instrument of a fate determined by God. I stand shaken before him. This is how he is: like a child, dear, good, compassionate; like a cat, cunning, clever and agile; like a lion, magnificently roaring and huge. A fine fellow, a real man.' Goebbels went on, 'Hitler's talk has the ring of prophecy. Above us in the sky a white cloud forms a swastika . . .' For the rest of his life – another nineteen years – Goebbels adored Hitler. It was as simple as that.

The *Second Book*

ADOLF HITLER'S *Second Book* was written in 1928 and, for a variety of reasons, was not published in his lifetime. In 1961 the Institute for Contemporary History in Munich published it as *Hitlers Zweites Buch: Ein Dokument aus dem Jahr 1928*. The English-language edition was published under the title *Hitler's Second Book: The Unpublished Sequel to Mein Kampf* in 2003 by Enigma Books of New York, edited and annotated by Gerhard Weinberg. It has sixteen chapters and 240 pages and covers much of the same ground as *Mein Kampf*. It covers potential foreign policy (it was written five years before he became Chancellor) and relationships with Britain and the British Empire, Italy, France (the inexorable enemy) and Russia (no alliance). Key individuals mentioned are Woodrow Wilson, US President from 1913 to 1921, Gustav Stresemann, co-founder of the German People's Party of 1918, Benito Mussolini, Fascist dictator of Italy, and Andreas Hofer, who founded a South Tyrol radical league.

'HERR HITLER THINKS OF A POLICY'

Hitler's heroes were mentioned many times – Otto von Bismarck, Frederick the Great, Napoleon I. His wilder flights of fancy include, 'The greatest danger to England will no longer be in Europe at all but in North America'; 'important English population centres appear virtually defenceless against French air attacks . . . and a French submarine war against England . . .' Predictably, there is his usual vilification of the Jews and Marxism.

Mein Kampf made Hitler a wealthy man. His *Second Book* did not earn him a single Reichsmark.

Short of Cash

When the Berghof, his Obersalzberg house, was being built, Hitler's architect, Albert Speer, costed the estimates and Hitler told him, 'I've completely used up the income from my book, although Amann's given me a further advance of several hundred thousand. Even so there's not enough money, so [Martin] Bormann has told me today. The publishers are after me to release my second book, the 1928 one, for publication [eventually published in 1961, sixteen years after the death of the author] . . . Perhaps later . . . Now it's impossible.'

The Horst Wessel Song

Goebbels, cruelly nicknamed by the Berliners '*der Krüppel*' (the cripple), was a brilliant publicist. In July 1927 he started his own newspaper *Der Angriff* (*The Attack*), first as a weekly, then a daily. It rapidly became a gutter press suitable for publicizing the Nazi Party. Every SA thug involved in a street brawl made headlines and Hitler read it from cover to cover every day. Early in 1930 a young agitator named Horst Wessel was shot by a Communist Party member possibly sent by a landlady whom he had not paid, and took six weeks to die. In Goebbels's paper

Wessel was called 'a socialist Christ'. At the spectacular funeral the Communists got into a pitched battle with the SA.

A few months before, Horst Wessel had written the lyrics for a new Nazi 'fighting song', which was published in September 1929 in *Der Angriff*. Translated, the lyrics read:

> 'The flags held high! The ranks stand firm together
> The SA marches with steady, resolute tread
> Soon Hitler's flags will fly over every street!'

It rapidly became the party anthem – sung to a melody said to be adapted from a Salvation Army hymn (the Salvation Army expanded into Germany in 1886), but which could equally be based on a North European folk tune – and took second place only to the national anthem, 'Deutschland, Deutschland Über Alles'.

'Like Ivy Around the Oak'

MARTIN BORMANN (1900–45) became one of the most powerful men in Hitler's Third Reich. In 1930 he founded the Nazi Party's fortunes by an ingenious scheme whereby millions of SA members paid a mandatory 30 pfennigs monthly and stuck stamps onto a yellow card, which gave them, or their family, life insurance in case of injury in street fighting and brawling with Communists and other opponents. He ran the Adolf Hitler Fund into which extorted funds and bribes, many from Jewish businessmen, were paid, and Hitler relied on him to deal with his money and property affairs. As Rudolf Hess's *chef de cabinet*, Bormann controlled access to the Führer, sometimes blocking even Goebbels, Göring, Speer and Himmler. Hitler's every whim or passing comment became a Führer command, elaborated, then circulated to the Party officials. A poor orator, Bormann remained in the background, and became indispensable, even though Hitler disapproved of his dealings with the Jews and the

Church. Robert Ley, a powerful, brutal Gauleiter and head of the DAF (*Deutsche Arbeitsfront*), said, 'Bormann clung to him [Hitler] like ivy around the oak, using him to get to the light and to the very summit.'

Staying at the Kaiserhof

IN SEPTEMBER 1930 Hitler achieved almost worldwide publicity. Tall, lumbering, half-American Putzi Hanfstängl placed three articles by Hitler in the US-based Hearst press. Hitler kept 70 per cent of the high fee (US $1,000) that each article commanded. The author was delighted. Now he could stay at the Berlin Kaiserhof Hotel – elegant and expensive. Moreover, he was interviewed by the London *Times* and sold an article to Britain's *Sunday Express*. At the dinner table on 6 July 1942 Hitler recalled, 'When I visited Berlin before we came to power [i.e. 1931–2] I used to stay at the Kaiserhof, accompanied by the complete General Staff. I booked a whole floor and our bill for food and lodging usually came to about ten thousand marks a week [actually 1,300 marks]. I earned enough to defray these costs mostly by means of interviews and articles for the foreign press. Towards the end of the "Struggle Period" [*Kampfzeit*] I was being paid as much as two or three thousand dollars a time for such work.' Rags to riches indeed.

'Corpse Tea'

AFTER HIS NIECE GELI'S DEATH in 1931 Hitler, for various reasons, did not touch meat, chicken, fish or eggs. He was obsessed by what he ate or did not eat and was a dedicated vegetarian. Or so we are told. He had a separate kitchen at the Berghof to provide his vegetarian meals. He lived mainly on pasta, mashed potatoes and green vegetables, and ended each meal with stewed fruit and mineral water. One of his favourite dishes was mashed potato laced with linseed oil and topped with grilled cheese, and he also liked corn-on the-cob and *Kaiserschmarrn*, a pudding with raisins soaked in sweet sauce. He usually drank apple or caraway tea, or freshly squeezed juice of fruit and vegetables from the Obersalzberg greenhouses – no alcohol apart from the occasional glass of watered sweet white wine. Two dieticians were employed by him to produce dishes for his irregular appetite and fads, but his favourite cook was Fräulein Constanze Manziarly from Innsbruck, who cooked Viennese and Bavarian dishes with skill. Albert Speer wrote that Hitler praised his diet cook and her vegetarian cuisine. Hitler described meat broth as 'corpse tea' and he would make fun of meat-eaters. However, in the 1930s Dione Lucas, a hotel chef in Hamburg, often prepared a special dish of stuffed squab (young pigeon) for Hitler. It is also possible that he was indulged by another of his cooks, huge, fat Willy Kanneneburg, with Bavarian sausages and *Leberknodl* (liver dumplings). Nevertheless in *Hitler's Table Talk,* on many occasions Hitler referred to his strict vegetarian food habits. How much his vegetarianism was due to Goebbels's propaganda machine is a moot point – and puzzling in that it was being peddled to a nation renowned for its sausage.

'The Price of Cheese'

WHEN HITLER WAS LOOKING for a property to buy, his choice was between the Berghof and one in Steingaden, a region famous for its cheeses. Of the latter he commented, 'If I had taken the place I should have been compelled to become a producer of the famous Steingaden cheese in order to keep the place up. Suppose the price of cheese went up? Everybody would immediately say "The Führer is himself personally interested in the price of cheese!"'

The Churchill Visit

IN 1932 Randolph Churchill, Winston's son, was a correspondent for *The Sunday Graphic* and visited Germany. On
Hitler's achievement of power in January 1933 the brash young
journalist sent a telegram to the Führer congratulating him on his
success, and persuaded his father, who was visiting the Blenheim
battlefield, that he should meet Hitler. So Winston Churchill
spent nearly a week at the Regina Hotel in Munich, where he met
Putzi Hanfstängl, Hitler's wealthy companion of the early 1920s.
Now, in 1933, he was foreign-press advisor to the Nazi Party.
Wealthy, with an American mother and American wife, Putzi
charmed the Churchills with his piano playing and familiar
English songs. Winston recalled, 'He said I ought to meet him
[Hitler] who came every day to the hotel about 5 o'clock and
would be very glad indeed to see me. I had no national prejudices
against Hitler at the time. I knew little of his doctrine or record
and nothing of his character. I admire men who stand up for their
country in defeat, even though I was on the other side.'

For a variety of not very convincing reasons, Hitler avoided a
meeting and Putzi later took him to task. 'You should have been
there. Among other things, Churchill sketched out the idea of an
alliance, with a request you should think about it.' Hitler replied
that Churchill was in (political) opposition and 'no one pays any
attention to him.' 'People say that same thing about you,' Putzi
retorted.

Hitler's Funding

THE ROYALTIES from *Mein Kampf* made Hitler wealthy, but
crafty, devoted Martin Bormann devised other sources of income.
In 1932 a *compulsory* accident insurance plan for Nazi Party
members produced considerable profits. With Hitler's approval,

his photographer Hoffman, his friend Karl Wilhelm Ohnesorge, Minister of Posts, and Bormann also ensured that Hitler earned a minute royalty on the tens of millions of postage stamps sold with his head on them. The Adolf Hitler Endowment Fund of German Industry was set up in the economic boom of the mid-1930s. Business leaders, particularly Jewish ones, were bluntly told to show their appreciation by *voluntary* contributions to the Führer. Dr Hjalmar Schacht, a financial wizard and ardent Nazi, paid for the Reich's expansion through what came to be called 'mefo' bills. These were credit notes issued in order to balance the books by a limited company (that existed in name only) called Metallurgische Forschungsgesellschaft – 'Mefo' for short. They served as bills of exchange, convertible into Reichsmarks upon demand, which were used mainly to pay armaments manufacturers.

Stateless

HITLER WAS BORN in Austria under the old Austro-Hungarian Empire, and was therefore legally an Austrian citizen. He formally renounced his citizenship in April 1925. In 1932 he stood for election to the Presidency of the German Republic, and thus urgently needed to become a legal German citizen. He was made Counsellor to the State of Brunswick legation in Berlin and swore loyalty to the Weimar Republic.

So for seven years Adolf Hitler was stateless.

The Chameleon – 'Multiplicity'

HITLER ARRIVED at the Berlin-Staaken airport on 27 July 1932 for a meeting, one of three scheduled for that day in the Brandenburg and Berlin stadiums. It was a very tight schedule. Albert Speer witnessed the arrival of the three aircraft and Hitler, associates and adjutants got out. Hitler reproved his companions because the cars had not yet arrived. He paced up and down slashing at the tops of his high boots with a dog whip, giving the impression of an uncontrolled man who treated his associates with contempt. He was 'very different from the man of calm and civilized manner who had so impressed me . . . I was seeing an example of Hitler's remarkable duplicity – indeed "multiplicity" would be a better word. With enormous histrionic intuition he could shape his behaviour to changing situations in public while letting himself go with his intimates, servants, or adjutants.'

The Unhappiest Woman in Germany

EVA BRAUN (1912–45) was born in Bavaria, at Simbach on the River Inn, close to the Austrian border. Although of limited convent-education, she was pretty, with a 'pudding face', and had a talent for dancing and amateur photography. She became an assistant in Heinrich Hoffmann's photographic studio in Amalienstrasse, Munich, where Hitler met her in 1929, two years before Geli's death. Eva set her cap at Hitler and slipped *billets-doux* into his pockets from time to time. On one occasion Geli discovered a message from Eva and her continuing jealousy possibly led to her suicide. Quite soon Eva became Hitler's mistress, installed in a Munich flat, but later she moved into the Berghof in Berchtesgaden. One of Hitler's chauffeurs, Erich Kempke, said years later that she was the unhappiest woman in Germany and spent most of her life waiting for Hitler. For company she often invited her sisters Ilse and Gretl to visit her. In 1944 it was arranged for Hermann Fegelein (eventually promoted to SS major-general) to marry Gretl, who was something of an embarrassment to Hitler. It also meant that Eva could come to official functions ostensibly with her sister and brother-in-law. Less than a year later, however, it seems that Hitler had Fegelein executed on suspicion of desertion.

After two years with Hitler Eva shot herself – the mirror image of Geli's suicide, or almost. Hitler was desperate and brought her flowers as she slowly recovered. After discussions with the doctor he told Hoffman, 'She did it for love of me. Now I must look after her; it mustn't happen again.'

Later, Eva wrote in her diary, 'I am so endlessly happy that he loves me so much and pray that it will always be so.' Nevertheless she tried to commit suicide a second time in 1935 with an overdose of (not too many) sleeping pills. Found by her sister, she was saved by a Jewish doctor who tactfully told Hitler that it was an accidental overdose brought on by tiredness. Eva attended the Nuremberg Rally in 1936 discreetly in the background. Hitler's Berghof became her gilded cage. The staff referred to her as 'EB', addressed her as 'Madame' and kissed her hand, and she called Hitler 'Chief'. Over the years they exchanged hundreds of letters.

Hitler and Suicide

HENRIETTE VON SCHIRACH – daughter of the photographer Heinrich Hoffman, a noted beauty whose name was once linked to Hitler's, was married to Baldur von Schirach, the head of the Hitler Youth movement. She wrote in 1952, 'I believe there are certain people who attract death and Hitler was definitely one of them.' Certainly he was in suicidal mode after the Beer Hall putsch of 1923 and the Strasser crisis of 1932, and probably after he ordered the execution of his friend Ernst Röhm during the 'Night of the Long Knives'. A girlfriend, Mimi Reiter, attempted suicide in 1926, Geli, his niece and mistress succeeded in 1931, Renate Müller, another friend, in 1937. Other suicides were Inge Ley, wife of Nazi politician Dr Robert Ley, Unity Mitford in

✠ ── ✠

1939 (she lingered until 1948) and Eva Braun, who was finally successful when she swallowed cyanide a few hours after her marriage to Hitler.

Gleichschaltung – the 'Synchronizing'

NINETEEN THIRTY-THREE was a wonderful year for Hitler. But it was a terrible year for Germany. It was the year of 'the co-ordination of the political will'. In January there were Nazi parades in Berlin and in February no fewer than thirty-three decrees were published banning rival political meetings or publications and dissolving the Prussian parliament. Communist Party offices were raided. On 27 February the Reichstag fire took place and Hitler was given emergency powers by presidential decree. In March Göring, on Hitler's orders, rounded up and imprisoned thousands of Communists and other opposition elements, and Dachau, the first concentration camp, was opened, to be followed by no fewer than fifty by the end of the year. The last free elections were held in March, with the Nazis getting 44 per cent of the vote. The SA, the Brownshirts, forced German state government resignations. Prussia had succumbed, now Bavaria was suppressed. Heinrich Himmler was made Bavarian Police President. Amnesties were granted to all Nazis who had committed crimes during the *Kampf* years of struggle. *Ermächtigungsgesetz* or Enabling Law was passed, giving Hitler extraordinary powers for the next four years. Goebbels was made Minister for Propaganda. The First Co-ordinations Law of States and Reich was passed, giving total control to the Chancellor. In April Jewish shops and professional men were boycotted. May saw all non-Nazi publications and all labour unions banned. That same month Goebbels organized the 'Burning of the Books', an outrageous act. In July the Nazis became the *only* legal party. In October

Hitler, who had become Chancellor in January, took Germany out of the League of Nations. In November the *Kraft durch Freude* ('Strength through Joy') movement was founded. The National Referendum in November showed that 95 per cent of the population approved Nazi policy.

It is unlikely that any sophisticated, civilized country in the world had surrendered their freedoms so quickly – and apparently so willingly – as in the year of *Gleichschaltung* or 'synchronizing', as the Nazi regime established and consolidated total control over the nation.

Um Blut und Boden – 'Blood and Earth'

ALTHOUGH HITLER all his life was an urban creature, he was a passionate advocate of 'blood and earth' policies. Abbreviated to *Blubo*, the word endorsed the primitive relationship of the German peasant (his blood) with the earth (*Boden*). Hitler had been influenced by Richard Walter Darré, an early Party member and friend who had written a book on the German peasantry, *Life Source of the Nordic Race*. Darré was appointed the Party's agricultural advisor and his peasant programme was published over Hitler's name on 6 March 1930. Besides economic aid for German farmers, there were state-credits, reduction and remission of taxes, higher protective tariffs, cheaper artificial manures, cheaper electricity and revision of inheritance laws. The tenor of the proposals was to emphasize the value of the peasantry and farming activities to the population as a whole. Darré organized Nazi farmworkers as the 'NS-Bauernschaft' in 1933. Hitler later said, 'Darré has done two good things: the law of agrarian inheritance and the regulation of markets.' Hitler set up a National Peasants' Assembly with a Harvest Festival, promotion of local and peasant art and the wearing of regional costumes, and encouraged 'Germanic' dances. The *Kreisbauernschaft* was a governmental agency authorized by Hitler to collect rural folklore, rituals, songs and dances. And he encouraged model villages and 'national peasant towns'.

The Demagogues

ALBERT SPEER had fifteen years of service with Hitler and Goebbels, the two main Nazi speech-makers, and wrote of them that they both understood how to unleash mass instincts at their meetings, how to play on the passions that underlie the veneer of ordinary respectable life. Practised demagogues, they succeeded in fusing the assembled workers, petits-bourgeois and students into a homogeneous mob whose opinions they could mould as they pleased. That was his opinion in 1930, but when Hitler came to power in 1933 things altered. Now the two politicians were in fact moulded by the mob itself, guided by its yearnings and daydreams. Of course Goebbels and Hitler knew how to penetrate to the instincts of their audiences, but in a deeper sense they derived their whole existence from these audiences. Certainly the crowds roared to the beat dictated by the batons of Hitler and Goebbels. Yet they were not the true conductors. The mob determined the theme. 'To compensate for misery, insecurity, unemployment and hopelessness, this anonymous assemblage wallowed for hours at a time in obsessions, savagery, licence. This was no ardent nationalism . . . Frenzy demanded victims. And Hitler and Goebbels threw them the victims.'

Hitler's Hour

WHEN HITLER BECAME Reich Chancellor in January 1933, the London *Daily Express* printed an article on 31 January headed 'Hitler's Hour'. It continued, 'What will he do now? . . . Mountebank or hero? There have been many who have called

'COMPULSORY SPONTANEOUS DEMONSTRATION'

Hitler either name. Events will now decide which of them history will fix on him.'

Gemütlichkeit

HITLER WAS BESIEGED by women after he became Chancellor. Hundreds of letters were sent to him every week. Women of all ages pursued him. He did not particularly want beauty, wit or class and he certainly would never have married a foreigner. What he wanted was *gemütlichkeit,* a domestic, non-threatening cosiness. 'A woman,' he declared, 'must be a cute, cuddly, naive little thing – tender, sweet and dim.'

Cartoons of the Führer

THE FÜHRER had a strange hobby – he collected the cartoons of himself that appeared frequently in the German press, certainly up until 1933, though more cautiously after that. With Hitler's permission Putzi Hanfstängl decided to use the cartoons for propaganda purposes, with a careful commentary explaining the myth behind the cartoonists' 'lies'. So a 174-page book appeared entitled *Hitler in der Karikatur des Welt* (*Hitler in the Cartoons of the World*), a picture compilation by Ernst Hanfstängl. Putzi of course had access to all cartoons published in the USA. Three editions appeared, in 1933, 1934 and 1938, and all the profits went to Putzi. Where are the original cartoons now?

The Reichstag Fire (1)

THE REICHSTAG BUILDING, a square stone structure with a dome and Corinthian columns, built in 1894, housed the parliament in Berlin. On 27 February 1933, a month after Hitler became Reich Chancellor, the building was burnt to the ground.

Hitler was dining that evening with Joseph and Magda Goebbels. Looking out of the window he could see flames in the sky above the Tiergarten and immediately cried, 'It's the Communists!' He and Goebbels set off at once to the blazing Reichstag where they found Hermann Göring busy saving the valuable Gobelin tapestries (which were his own private property). Since August 1932 he had been President of the Reichstag and was then living in the old Prussian presidential palace nearby. As if on cue, Göring shouted, 'This is the start of a Communist uprising. Not a moment must be lost.' Hitler went into overdrive. 'Now we'll show them. Anyone who stands in our way will be mown down. The German people have been soft too long. All Communist deputies must be hanged this very night. All friends of the Communists must be locked up . . .' Immediately the SA arrested 4,000 leading Communists, plus many Social Democrats and liberals, including Reichstag members normally immune from arrest. An arsonist, a simple-minded young Dutch Communist, Marinus van der Lubbe, was charged and after imprisonment and trial was beheaded. Forensic evidence showed that the fire had been so professionally started in various parts of the building that one man alone could not have done it; van der Lubbe had clearly been given expert help. The show trial in Leipzig in September acquitted the leading Communists – Torgeler, Dimitrov and many others. Göring, *Der Dicke* ('the fat one') as the Berliners called him, stormed and ranted at the trial and was ridiculed in the world's press. It seemed almost as though the Nazis were on trial.

The Reichstag Fire (2) The Plot and Aftermath

THE PROBABILITY REMAINS that Hitler wanted to wipe out the hundred or so Communist seats among the 600 deputies in the Reichstag. Hitler controlled 250 seats, which was not quite overall control of the house. So he had a word with Hermann

Göring, his deputy and Prussian Minister of the Interior, who had a word with Reinhard Heydrich's SS intelligence department (*Sicherheitsdienst*) and on the night of 27 February the SD agents secretly entered the Reichstag through an underground tunnel that connected Göring's official residence to a cellar in the parliament. After the fire Hitler persuaded President Hindenburg to sign a decree 'for the Protection of the People and State', an order suspending civil liberties and freedom of expression. In the March elections, after a media frenzy by Goebbels and the imprisonment of the Communist deputies, Hitler's Nazi Party gained 5 million votes with 44 per cent of the poll. With yet another 'Law for the Removal of Distress of People and Reich' Hitler gained control of parliament.

Hitler's Silver Arrows

THE MAGNIFICENT German automobile industry owes its fame partially to Hitler's dynamism and love of cars. In 1933 he personally proposed to Dr Ferdinand Porsche his idea of a small and affordable car – the Volkswagen ('the people's car'). Porsche had already been working on something similar for a few years, and he had two prototypes working in 1935. 'After the war,' Hitler said in June 1942, 'the Volkswagen will become the car par excellence for the whole of Europe . . . it is air-cooled, and so unaffected by any winter conditions. I should not be surprised to see the annual output reach anything from a million to a million and a half.' Hitler praised Porsche, whom he called 'the greatest engineer in Germany. He has the courage to give his ideas [time] to ripen.' Hitler and the Nazi Party provided funds for Auto Union and Mercedes-Benz to produce the superb Silver Arrows, D-type 3-litre 485-bhp racers, which dominated the Grand Prix in the 1930s (and later). They reached 250 mph during land-speed record runs. Hitler, who was devoted to automobiles – speed and danger – met many of the triumphant German racing drivers. In 1937 he awarded Dr Porsche the country's National Prize for Art and Science.

Sea Cruises for All

IN APRIL 1933 Hitler had been Chancellor for three months of a bankrupt economy and huge unemployment. He banned the Communist Party – all 6 million of them – and introduced strict price and wage controls. He closed down all trade unions and in 1934 merged them into the DAF (German Labour Front) with 30 million members – the largest trades union in the world. The DAF funded the Volkswagen factory, food factories, a German Labour Bank, housing schemes, hotels for workers' holidays and convalescence homes for sick workers. Holiday-cruise liners were provided so that workers could see the outside world (but to Europe only). The DAF regularly received 95 per cent of subscriptions due, which showed how popular Hitler's plans were for the workers. The armed forces quickly doubled, then tripled in size, thus diminishing the unemployment problem. The DAF was an astonishing success. Hitler wrote, 'In future every worker will have his holidays – a few days in each year which he can arrange as he likes. And everybody will be able to go on a sea cruise once or twice in his life.'

The 'Brown Pages'

THE *Forschungsamt* (FA) wire taps were important security measures introduced by Hitler to control his police state. This so-called 'Research Office' – the Reich's spy network – was set up in April 1933 and controlled by Hermann Göring. The wire taps, printed on unusual brown paper, were sent in locked despatch boxes or by pneumatic post direct to carefully chosen ministers.

Some of those known to be spied on included Hitler's adjutant, Fritz Wiedemann, Gauleiter Julius Streicher, Goebbels's several mistresses, Princess Stephanie Hohenlohe and Unity Mitford. Polish, Czech, French, British, Italian, Japanese and Belgian diplomats were routinely tapped, as were the British and US Embassies in Berlin. The London *Times* correspondent and the church leader, Pastor Martin Niemöller, were also 'bugged'.

Later, Churchill had the daily German Enigma reports intercepted by ULTRA. Hitler had his FA wire taps, daily recording telephone calls between key 'targets' in Germany who were communicating externally to London, New York, Paris and Moscow.

Hitler's SS Bodyguard

In 1933, just after the Reichstag fire, the Reichsführer SS, Heinrich Himmler, 'discovered' two secret plots against Hitler's life. One was led by by Count Arco-Valley, the other by three Soviet agents who had supposedly hidden grenades for Hitler's car to drive over. Himmler also put up another smokescreen of 'French attempts on the life of the Chancellor of the Reich'. Hitler lived in constant fear of being assassinated, so he asked Himmler to set up a special guard of SS for his personal security. Thus was formed the Führer's personal bodyguard, the Leibstandarte SS Adolf Hitler ('Adolf Hitler's SS Bodyguard Regiment'), under Joseph 'Sepp' Dietrich, who was later promoted to SS General and became Hitler's favourite soldier.

Arisierung or Aryanization

Many of the 525,000 or so Jews in pre-war Germany who owned businesses, factories and shops were targeted by Nazi hooliganism. The first Nazi boycott of all Jewish shops and businesses was personally planned by Hitler for 1 April 1933.

This repression was supervised by the SA General Julius Streicher. Shop windows were covered with anti-Semitic slogans and clients who tried to enter were physically bullied. The historian Saul Friedlander has pointed out, however, that it became increasingly clear to Hitler himself that Jewish economic life was not to be openly interfered with, at least not for as long as the German economy was still in a precarious position. Indeed, as late as 1938 the powerful Dresdener Bank still had five Jewish directors, and there were three Jews among the eight directors of the German Central Bank.

The second phase of persecution was that all 5,000 Jewish civil servants were fired, and 30 per cent of the 4,585 Jewish lawyers were ejected from the National Association of Lawyers. Jewish musicians, actors, film producers, boxers and doctors were soon disbarred, threatened or dismissed.

The Führer's Paladin

HERMANN GÖRING, given the special title of Reichsmarschall and named as Hitler's successor, was terrified of Hitler and confessed to the banker Hjalmar Schacht, 'Every time I stand before the Führer, my heart falls into my trousers.' But when the Nazi Party took power in 1933 he declared, 'No title and no distinction can make me as happy as the designation bestowed on me by the German people, "The most faithful paladin of the Führer."'

Unity – Stalking Hitler

THE HON. UNITY VALKYRIE MITFORD, known as 'Bobo' to her family, may have been Hitler's lover. She was certainly a very close friend in the four-year period 1935–39, when they met on no fewer than 180 occasions. She was born in 1919, tried to commit suicide twice, and ultimately died from the effects of the second attempt in 1948. She was a strapping blonde girl nearly six foot tall, with large, pale blue eyes. A tremendous show-off who enjoyed startling people with her peculiar pets – a rat and a snake – she was also a great giggler and attracted the young Randolph Churchill. With her sister Diana she visited Nuremberg in 1933 and admired the Nazi Party and its leader on display. On her return to England Unity attended Sir Oswald Mosley's British Union of Fascists rallies, proudly wearing a black shirt, and sold copies of the *Blackshirt* magazine from the BUF office in Oxford. She persuaded her parents to let her spend a year in Germany at finishing school in Munich to learn the language. She stayed with Baroness Laroche at 121 Königinstrasse and worked hard on her German language studies, wearing a black shirt and BUF badge to classes. Having made up her mind that she wanted to meet Hitler, she discovered that he often lunched at the restaurant Osteria Bavaria and had tea at the Carlton tearooms. In June 1934 she saw Hitler in the tearooms, but did not meet him on that occasion. Her sister, Nancy Mitford, caricatured Unity in her novel *Wigs on the Green* as 'Eugenia', a Fascist activist.

Hitler's Architectural Sketches

According to Speer Hitler perpetually made sketches which, although tossed off casually, were accurate in perspective. He drew outlines, cross-sections and renderings to scale which could not have been done better by an architect. Sometimes he would show Speer a well-executed sketch he had prepared overnight, but more often his drawings were done in a few hasty strokes during their discussions. Speer kept 125 of Hitler's 'quick' sketches, a quarter of which related to the 'Linz Project' (comprising a museum, library, theatre, and so on), which was always close to Hitler's heart, and many of them were sketches for theatres.

The English Court

LEOPOLD VON HOESCH, the German Ambassador in London, sent a despatch, No. A2705, headed 'Subject: German-English relations' on 16 August 1933 back to the Foreign Minister in Berlin, Baron Konstantin von Neurath, and thence to Hitler. Part of it read, 'We must mention the English Court where true sympathy for Germany is still to be found. To be sure King George [V] has become more and more critical in his attitude towards the German revolution and various statements which I know him to have made recently are in fact anything but friendly. On the other hand the Queen [Mary, who was German by birth] and various princes and princesses who are connected by family ties with Germany still entertain a warm feeling for our people and country and also a certain sympathy, or at any rate a lively interest in the most recent German developments. Most pronounced are the sympathies and the interest in the case of the successor to the throne the Prince [of Wales, briefly King Edward VIII from January to December 1936], with whom I have often had opportunities for a frank and detailed discussion.'

Edward VIII was bilingual in German, speaking it regularly with his mother and earlier with Kaiser Wilhelm II, 'Uncle Willi', his favourite uncle. As the Duke of Windsor after his abdication he continued his friendship with the Nazi regime.

Hitler's Appearance – a Masculine Viewpoint

WILLIAM SHIRER, the American CBS journalist in Berlin for much of the pre-war period and until December 1940, expected on arrival to see a 'mad, brutish dictator'. Instead he found a man with a 'rather common' face. 'It was coarse. It was not particularly strong. Sometimes when he was obviously fatigued from the long speeches, the hours spent in reviewing his troops, it appeared flabby . . . He was about five feet, nine inches tall and weighed around 150 pounds. His legs were short and his knees turned in slightly so that he seemed to be a bit knock-kneed. He had well-formed hands with long graceful fingers that reminded one of those of a concert pianist, and he used them effectively . . . in gestures during a speech or when talking informally with a small group. His nose betrayed the brutal side of him. It was straight but rather large and broadened at the base, where thick nostrils widened it . . . His mouth was quite expressive, and it could reflect a variety of moods.'

Strength Through Joy – the Master Race

Kraft durch Freude or 'Strength through Joy' was first proposed to Hitler by Dr Robert Ley, leader of the German Labour Front (DAF) in 1933. Based on the funds confiscated from the original trade unions, an immense business was created to finance the *Kraft durch Freude*. It was an imitation of Mussolini's *dopo lavoro* or *nach der arbeit* ('after work'). But Hitler had already adopted some of the philosophies of Nietzsche, who praised strength and denounced weakness in trenchant prose. From 1880 to 1914 the *Arbeiterturnerbund* (Workers' Gymnastic Association) had encouraged millions of Germans to engage in physical education. It and the upmarket *Deutsche Turnerschaft* had together reached two and a half million members. Sports and games were introduced from Britain: football, tennis, swimming, water polo, boxing, wrestling, athletics, rowing and mountaineering (but not cricket). Hitler even approved of women boxing and wrestling. His SA organized its own Sports Badge and Reich Sports contests. From 1933 subsidized holidays, sports facilities, cruises, dancing, concerts, films, exhibitions, theatre and concerts were all designed by Hitler to raise the physical fitness of the nation – not necessarily for peaceful purposes. But he himself said, 'People sometimes ask me why I play no games. The answer is simple. I'm no good at games, and I refuse to make a fool of myself!'

Hitler – the Riddle

SIR MAURICE HANKEY, Secretary to the British Cabinet, wrote on 24 October 1933, 'Are we still dealing with the Hitler of *Mein Kampf* lulling his opponents to sleep with fair words in order to gain time to arm his people? . . . Or is it a new Hitler who has discovered the burden of responsible office? That is the riddle that has to be solved.' Hitler had ten days before withdrawing Germany from the League of Nations. The British government was not able to assess the new regime in Germany despite excellent informative reports from Sir Horace Rumbold, the British Ambassador in Berlin.

'Frightfully Stiff and Bombastic'

STEPHANIE VON HOHENLOHE, née Richter (1891–1972) became a princess by marrying Prince Friedrich von Hohenlohe in Westminster in May 1914. She was a citizen of the Austro-Hungarian Empire and most of her lovers were powerful and influential men. By 1932 she had persuaded her friend, Lord Rothermere, the newspaper proprietor, to give her a three-year contract as his agent, which remained in force until 1938 and earned her over £1 million in today's money. She travelled to Hungary, the Netherlands and Germany, and in 1937 became the mistress of Hitler's adjutant, Friedrich Wiedemann, Hitler's company commander in the Great War. In December 1933 she met Hitler and handed over a letter from Lord Rothermere suggesting a meeting. His *Daily Mail*, a mass-circulation newspaper, often carried articles about the virtues of Nazi Germany. The Führer wore his usual fawn military-style jacket, a white shirt, brown tie fastened with a swastika tie-pin and black uniform trousers, plus black socks and black patent leather gloves. Princess Stephanie thought he looked like a minor clerk, and very neat and tidy. Hitler kissed her on the hand and gave her tea, but Stephanie, a Viennese and a dedicated social snob, thought that his Austrian accent was 'of the lowest class like someone who is trying to express himself in a language that he is not born to. Frightfully stiff and bombastic.' Returning to London with Hitler's letter, Rothermere's 'agent' was paid a bonus of £2,000, and a strong pro-Hitler campaign appeared in the press baron's newspapers.

The Blood Purge (1)

ON 30 JUNE 1934 a 'second revolution' was plotted by Hitler's old friend Ernst Röhm, chief of the brown-shirted SA. That day came to be known as the 'blood purge' or the 'Night of the Long Knives'. The SA had 4½ million members, mainly rough, unemployed ex-soldiers, who frequented Munich beer halls. Their uniform, raised-arm salute and swastika derived from the recently disbanded Freikorps. Frequently the SA clashed with Himmler's elite 100,000-strong *Schutzstaffel*, the SS. Hitler's close supporters, Göring, Werner von Blomberg (Minister of Defence), Himmler, Reinhard Heydrich, Werner Best and Victor Lutze (an SA leader who wanted to oust Röhm), all urged him to act against the SA. Hitler flew to Munich with Goebbels at dawn on 30 June in Operation Colibri, drove to Bad Weisee and arrested Röhm and other SA leaders. The Stadelheim prison was crammed with SA prisoners. Operation Hummingbird was the signal for Göring in Berlin to take the local SA leaders to Lichterfelde army cadet school, where they were all shot. Hitler had his good friend Röhm shot in his prison cell by Theodor Eicke on 1 July. In the massacre former Reich Chancellor

General von Schleicht and his wife, Gregor Strasser, a key radical Nazi and another of Hitler's friends, Edmund Heines, Nazi boss of Silesia, Dr Erich Klausner and Gustav von Kahe were all slaughtered. In his speech in the Reichstag on Friday, 13 July, Hitler screamed, 'The supreme court of the German people during those twenty-four hours consisted of myself.' He claimed that 'only' nineteen senior and forty-two other SA men had been shot, plus thirteen 'resisting arrest'; and three had committed suicide. In the 'Röhm purge' probably more than a thousand were killed, mostly SA but also others for the sake of vengeance.

As for Hitler – he said to his loyal secretary, Christa Schröder, 'So! Now I have taken a bath and feel clean as a newborn babe again.'

The Times and Hitler

In 1931 Geoffrey Dawson, editor of *The Times,* met Alfred Rosenberg, who had joined Hitler's movement in 1920 and become editor of the Nazi Party's own newspaper, the *Völkischer Beobachter*. Rosenberg impressed Hitler with his views on racialism and Communism and with his similar philosophy. He wrote 'The Future Course of German Foreign Policy' and played host in Germany to a number of eminent British people, including several peers, two generals, an admiral and a number of journalists. In 1933, while Göring and his stormtroopers bullied the electorate and Goebbels's persuasive propaganda was in full flow, *The Times* carefully wrote, 'No one doubts Herr Hitler's sincerity. That nearly 12 million Germans follow him blindly says much for his personal magnetism.'

When Hitler withdrew Germany from the Disarmament Conference in Geneva and from the League of Nations in October 1933, Geoffrey Dawson pleaded 'The German Case' in *The Times*, arguing that their impatience had been understandable and 'Hitler should be given the chance of showing that he is something more than an orator and an agitator'. Even after the infamous 'Night of the Long Knives' on 30 June 1934, *The Times* drew the conclusion that 'during the next few years there is more reason to be afraid for Germany, than to be afraid of Germany.'

The Blood Purge (2)

TEN YEARS AFTER the 'blood purge' of 1933 Hitler recounted to Speer how excited he had been in the days following the SA massacres; how he had forced his way into the Hotel Hanselbauer in Wiesee. 'We were unarmed, imagine, and didn't know whether or not those swine might have armed guards to use against us . . . In one room we found two naked boys in bed [Heines and friend, who were both shot]. I alone was able to solve this problem [quelling the putsch]. No one else!' The newspapers reported that President Hindenburg had officially praised Chancellor Hitler and Prussian Prime Minister Hermann Göring for their prompt action. Hitler was overjoyed: 'When circumstances require it, one must not shrink from the most extreme action. One must be able to spill blood also.'

One interesting theory is that Stalin in the Kremlin, where the 'Röhm purge' was greeted with approval, had instigated rumours through the Soviet intelligence service about Röhm's intentions. Röhm favoured an alliance with France rather than with the USSR, which was not what Stalin wanted.

Göring's Assurance – 'No Enemy Planes'

THE KEY SHOWPIECE in the grandiose Hitlerian plan for the future, Adolf Hitler Platz in Berlin, was to be the great domed hall – an assembly chamber for 1,200 deputies, representing a future Germanic population of 140 million. It would hold over

150,000 standing people, have a diameter of 825 feet and rise to a height of 726 feet. The interior would be sixteen times greater in volume than St Peter's in Rome. The dome would be crowned by an eagle with a swastika. The Reich Air Ministry was told of the plans for a building that would act as an ideal navigational guide to enemy bombers, but Hitler answered their fears, 'Göring has assured me that no enemy plane will enter Germany. We will not let that sort of thing stand in the way of our plans.'

'Sepp' – 'Cunning, Energetic and Brutal'

JOSEF 'SEPP' DIETRICH (1892–1966) was Hitler's favourite soldier. A sergeant-major in the Great War, he was a typical early Nazi street-brawler and bully-boy. He fought with the Freikorps in 1919 and in 1928 joined the Nazi Party, soon becoming a full-time commander of Hitler's SS bodyguard. On 3 January 1942, the Führer described Sepp: 'The role of Dietrich is unique. I've always given him opportunity to intervene at sore spots. He's a man who's simultaneously cunning, energetic and brutal. Under his swashbuckling appearance, Dietrich is a serious, conscientious, scrupulous character. And what care he takes of his troops! He's a phenomenon in the class of people like Frundsberg, Ziethen and Seydlitz. He's a Bavarian Wrangel, someone irreplaceable. For the German people, Sepp Dietrich is a national institution! For me personally, there's also the fact that he is one of my oldest companions in the struggle.'

Dietrich later became an SS major-general in charge of the elite Leibstandarte Adolf Hitler which did special execution work in the Röhm purge of 1934. He fought in France, Greece, Russia and commanded the 1 SS Panzer Corps in Normandy in 1944 and the Sixth SS Panzer Army in the Ardennes Battle of the Bulge in mid-winter 1944–5. His much reduced army was sent to defend Vienna in spring 1945 and when it was overwhelmed by the

Russian juggernaut, Hitler dismissed him in a rage. He was fortunate to survive and, despite prison sentences, to live until April 1966.

Hitler's Films

GOEBBELS OFTEN PRESENTED selections of films to his Führer. These were shown in the music salon in the Reich Chancellery or in the Berghof. Every evening a crude movie projector was set up to show a newsreel and one or two films. Usually Hitler wanted two films every evening and made running comments, often vetoing a film half way through and walking out in disgust. He favoured light entertainment, love and society films but not comedies (Chaplin and Buster Keaton were out). Two of his favourites were *Mutiny on the Bounty* and *The Hound of the Baskervilles*. Films with Emil Jannings, Heinz Rühmann, Henny Porten, Lil Dagover and Jenny Jugo were popular, and Mickey Mouse cartoons and revues with lots of leg on display were often shown. He was a self-confessed fan of Shirley Temple and Jeanette MacDonald, and 'Donkey Serenade' was his favourite Hollywood movie tune.

Rassenkunde – Racial-Science Brainwashing

HITLER, who had never forgiven those who had refused him entry to the Academy of Fine Arts Vienna, had a withering contempt for schoolteachers and academic institutions. Education, he wrote in *Mein Kampf*, 'must aim primarily not at the stuffing with mere knowledge but at building bodies which are physically healthy to the core' and training them to serve 'a new national state'. To this end, Hitler made an unemployed provincial schoolteacher, Obergruppenführer Dr Bernhard Rust, former Gauleiter of Hanover (dismissed on grounds of 'mental instability'), the Minister for Education. Rust's boast was that he was 'liquidating the school as an institution of intellectual acrobats'. His job was to 'Nazify' the educational system. For a long time Germany had had a magnificent reputation for its fine universities and schools. In the first five years of Hitler's rule very nearly 3,000 professors and instructors at universities were dismissed – a quarter of the total. University enrolment reduced in six years from 127,920 to 58,325. At the institutes of technology the number of scientists and engineers fell from 20,474 to 9,554. The University of Berlin under the new rector soon had five new courses – in racial science.

Pecking Order

BETWEEN 1 and 10 January 1934 Hitler published a series of 'thank-you notes' in 'his' paper, the *Völkischer Beobachter*. The pecking order at that time was Hess, Schwarz (Nazi Party Treasurer), Max Amann, Himmler, Röhm, Goebbels and Rosenberg. Then followed Göring, Robert Ley, Baldur von Schirach (head of the Hitler Youth Movement), Walter Buch (Chairman of the USCHLA, the Nazi disciplinary court), Franz Seldte (leader of the Stahlhelm, the militant ex-servicemen's association) and finally Richard Walter Darré (organizer of the NS-Bauernschaft Nazi farmworkers, who became Minister of Food and Agriculture). It is interesting that Göring, listed eighth, became Hitler's successor-designate.

A Pipeline to Buckingham Palace

LEOPOLD VON HOESCH, the German Ambassador in London in the early 1930s, was entertained at Windsor Castle on 25 April 1934 by King George V, Queen Mary, the Duke of Kent (Prince George) and other members of the royal family. Hoesch reported back to Berlin: 'The King engaged me in a long political conversation, and did not hesitate to express some adverse criticism of the dictated peace of Versailles [music to Hoesch's ears]. In this connection he made the war itself [the Great War] as a human madness, responsible for such deplorable consequences.' King George went on to say that 'as long as he was living, England would not again become involved in war. Accordingly, out of his firm conviction that a new war would mean the ruin of everybody, he would do everything in his power to forestall every possibility of war.'

The royal family's cousins in St Petersburg had been swept away in the Russian Revolution so there was no love of Bolsheviks in Windsor Castle. And it was clear that Hitler's main object was to defeat Bolshevism. No wonder Rosenberg reported to his master, Adolf Hitler, that there was 'a pipeline to Buckingham Palace'.

The Swastika 'Blood Flag' and the Thousand-Year Reich

THE NUREMBERG RALLY that started on 4 September 1934 was beautifully and frighteningly organized. In the huge Luitpold hall there were almost 30,000 Nazi Party supporters. Hitler had brought pageantry back to Germany. A large symphony orchestra played the Badenweiler March, a military march composed by Georg Fürst for the Royal Bavarian Infantry Regiment during the Great War, which was a favourite of Hitler's and was now played only when the Führer was involved in a special occasion. Hitler appeared in the back of the auditorium followed by Hermann Göring, Joseph Goebbels, Rudolf Hess and Heinrich Himmler – the five individuals who controlled the Third Reich. All were dressed in brown uniforms except Himmler, who was in the black garb of the SS. As soon as the Nazi chiefs were seated on the huge platform backed by the swastika 'blood flag' of the 1923 Beer Hall putsch, and 500 SA flag-standards, the orchestra played Beethoven's *Egmont* Overture. Great klieg lights played on the stage as Rudolf Hess, the tall, strong, brutal deputy to Hitler, slowly read out the names of the Nazi so-called 'martyrs' who had been killed during the putsch. Hitler was saving his voice as he was scheduled to give seven speeches during the rally so Adolf Wagner, regional Party leader, or Gauleiter, of Bavaria, read out the Führer's speech to the 30,000 faithful. 'The German form of life is definitely determined for the next thousand years. For us, the nervous nineteenth century has finally ended. There will be no revolution in Germany for the next one thousand years.'

More Hitler Cartoons

IN SEPTEMBER 1934 Putzi Hanfstängl had his second book published, which contained refutations of the adverse Hitler cartoons emanating from the world's press. It was called *Tat gegen Tinte* ('Fact versus Ink') and was a mixture of satire and humour with themes such as 'Hitler der Friedensstörer' (Hitler the Troublemaker) and 'Hitler der Terrorist' and the rather convoluted (translated) 'Hitler as Cultural Reactionary, Suppressor of Culture, and Racist Politician'. A postscript to the book carried the friendly assurance that it had been read and approved by the Führer.

The Turkish Whore

PUTZI HANFSTÄNGL had an important PR meeting at dinner on 27 April 1933 with Louis Lochner (Associated Press), his aristocratic wife, Hilde, General Wilhelm Groener, the US Consul-General George Messersmith, and other bigwigs. Putzi refused to wear a Nazi Party uniform and ordered a chocolate-brown gabardine cloth from a London tailor to be made up into a uniform with delicate gold epaulettes. Putzi thought he looked terrific. Hitler, however, was appalled, 'You look like a Turkish whore,' he said.

The 'Garrulous Monk'

THE FIRST TIME that the two European dictators, Benito Mussolini and Adolf Hitler, met was on 14 June 1934 in the Royal Villa at Stra, near Padua. The Führer was surrounded by a cohort of fully armed SS men led by 'Sepp' Dietrich. Mussolini was profoundly unimpressed. He noted Hitler's lank, ill-brushed hair and watery eyes, and his yellow mackintosh, striped trousers and patent-leather shoes. Mussolini, of course – *bella figura* – as a proper Duce, was wearing a splendid Fascist uniform with ceremonial dagger and black boots with silver spurs. They conversed in German (Mussolini spoke several languages) and agreed that they both disliked Russia and France. Austria was, however, a bone of contention as it was in Mussolini's interest that Austria – where the Nazis were using 'terrorist' tactics – should remain independent. The conference transferred to Venice, where Hitler spouted much of his *Mein Kampf* from memory to the bored Duce, who after the meeting expressed his contempt for the 'silly little clown' and 'the garrulous monk'.

Rival Factions

AFTER 1933 – the watershed – the main players developed their own cliques, but not a power base. Goebbels surrounded himself with literary and cinema stars, producers and, particularly, actresses. Hess had interesting acquaintances, enjoyed chamber music and delved into homeopathic medicines. Himmler became almost a deity among his brutalized SS hierarchy. His missionary zeal (he initially recruited sons of princes and counts) made him feel superior to the others. 'Der Grosse' Hermann Göring entertained his large family and Luftwaffe friends lavishly at Carinhall, his country residence, and one way and another he became very rich; during the war he looted the art treasures of Europe. Hitler held these four divergent groups together politically, for the only thing they had in common was the success of the Third Reich and their fear of the Führer's power.

The Perfect Goose-Step

HITLER'S LABOUR SERVICE CORPS, his *Arbeitsdienst*, was launched to the German public at Nuremberg on 6 September 1934. Fifty thousand highly trained, semi-military young men – fanatical Nazi youths – were on parade in the early-morning sunlight. Instead of guns they bore shiny spades. The first thousand were bared to the waist and without warning they broke into a perfect goose-step, strutting proudly. This struck an inner chord in the soul of the German people and the tens of thousands of spectators jumped up spontaneously and shouted their applause. The Labour Service boys then formed an immense *Sprechchor* – a chanting, shouting chorus intoning, 'We want one Leader! Nothing for us! Everything for Germany! Heil Hitler!' A few years later these proud young goose-steppers marched their way through Poland, the Low Countries and France.

Duke of Linz, Perhaps?

HITLER THOUGHT all kings were monumentally stupid. To his dinner companions on 5 July 1942, he recounted, 'About a year after the victory of our Party, one of our former potentates, [Prince] Rupprecht of Bavaria, sent an emissary to me to say that he was sure I would recognize the necessity of restoring the monarchy [in Germany]. The emissary, following his instructions, went on to say quite frankly that I could not, of course, remain as Reich Chancellor in the restored monarchy because my continued presence would be an obstacle to the unification of the German people. I should however be most generously treated and should be rewarded – with a dukedom!' Duke of Linz, perhaps? He went on, 'The idiot imagined that some confounded nincompoop could tempt me to give up the leadership of this great people – by making me a duke!'

Hitler – Mickey Mouse Fan

IN THE MID AND LATE 1930s Goebbels controlled the film and theatre production in Germany. He censored and rated for tax purposes every film, and read film scripts nearly every evening. Hitler and he were passionate fans of cinematic art. In one year Goebbels gave Hitler thirty serious films and eighteen Mickey Mouse cartoons as Christmas presents.

Hitler's Tax Returns

HITLER'S ANNUAL TAX RETURNS from 1924 to 1935 can be seen either in the Bavarian State Archives or the Alderman Library of the University of Virginia, USA. They comprise some 200 items. A full analysis is contained in O. J. Hale's article, 'Adolf Hitler, Taxpayer', in *The American Historical Review* of July 1955. Hitler described himself to the tax authorities as 'writer' and was liable for income tax, turnover tax (*umsatzsteuer*) on sales of *Mein Kampf* and property tax (*vermögenssteur*). Julius Schaub negotiated on behalf of Hitler, usually with Fritz Reinhardt, a long-term Nazi, who was Secretary of State to the Reich Ministry of Finance.

Game, Set and Match

AFTER A YEAR as Reich Chancellor and Führer, Hitler, who was delinquent with his annual tax returns put fairly discreet pressure on the Ministry of Finance. As a result, on 19 December 1934, confirmed on 25 February 1935, a memorandum from Dr Lizius, chief of the Finance Office, Munich-East, noted, 'The order to declare the Führer tax-exempt was therefore final. Thereupon I withdrew all the Führer's records, including the tax cards, from official circulation and placed them under lock and key.' Game, set and match to the tax-exempt Führer.

The Mitford Girls: 'Sitting beside the Sun'

THE TWO GOOD-LOOKING DAUGHTERS of Lord Redesdale, Unity Mitford and her sister Diana, met Hitler in 1935, when he warned them of 'the Jewish and Bolshevik dangers'. They both fell under his spell, Unity remarking that sitting next to Hitler was 'like sitting beside the sun'. Diana was in the throes of divorcing Bryan Guinness, by whom she had two sons, and marrying the leader of the British Union of Fascists, Sir Oswald Mosley, an admirer of Mussolini and a notorious womanizer. At her second wedding, guests included Hitler and Goebbels (who found the Mitfords 'boring as ever'), which horrified the Mitford family and scandalized British society. Unity Mitford became a member of the Hitler social group, with Albert Speer, the photographer Heinrich Hoffmann and Martin Bormann. One tacit agreement which prevailed at the tipsy lunches (the Osteria Bavaria, Munich was a favourite) was that no one must mention politics, except for Unity, who pleaded with Hitler to make a deal with England. In September 1939, when Britain declared war on Germany, Unity shot herself with a small pistol in, appropriately, Munich's Englischer Garten.

Hitler recalled in August 1942: 'Churchill and his friends decided on war against us some years before 1939. I had this information from Lady [*sic*] Mitford; she and her sisters were very much in the know, thanks to their relationship with influential people.'

The Mosleys were arrested in England and detained for three and a half years.

Paula Hitler

HITLER'S YOUNGER SISTER PAULA (1896–1960) lived mainly in Vienna, where she ran an arts-and-crafts shop. When her brother Adolf became famous, or notorious, she changed her name to Wolf. She never married and from 1935 she occasionally acted as housekeeper at the Berghof. Hitler made her an allowance of 250 marks per month and in 1938 increased it to 500 marks. At Christmas he would often give her money and also helped her buy a villa. He also left her money in his will.

Hitler on Motherhood

HITLER WANTED to increase the Aryan population of Germany. While, one way or another, he drove out the Jews and Romanies, he led a big drive for motherhood. He outlawed abortion, forbade campaigns to promote contraception, instituted a system of marriage loans (a certificate of 1,000 Reichmarks for a couple to buy furniture) and made it compulsory for husbands to leave their property to their wives and children. Since motherhood was the highest calling for German women they must also be physically strong, like the Valkyries of legend. The *Bund Deutscher Mädl* was formed for all girls from the age of fourteen (those under that age joined the *Jungmädel*). A new ideal of 'Aryan maidenhood' was drawn up which included

✠ ⸻⸻⸻⸻⸻⸻⸻⸻⸻⸻⸻⸻⸻ ✠

physical prowess and an outdoor 'natural' life that would include a year of farm or domestic service. So the fit young girls became fit young brides and fit young mothers.

The Führer Niche

IN THE 1930s the popular admiration for Hitler was at its zenith. The vast majority of Germans now venerated him thanks to his powerful rhetoric on the radio and at Nazi rallies. Goebbels kept up a never-ending barrage of media adulation. All the attributes of a superman were ascribed to Hitler. His physical unapproachability enhanced his prestige. The cult of the Führer found expression in the letters and presents that daily arrived for him. In the eyes of many Germans, particularly the women, Hitler as a substitute for God stood above basic earthly concerns. If there were any perceived evils, shocks or horrors it must have been because the Führer knew nothing about them. Many households set up in their living room, in place of a religious shrine, a 'Führer niche' with his picture surrounded by flowers.

Hitler's Oratory

ALBERT SPEER described Hitler's gift for oratory: how in a low voice, hesitantly and somewhat shyly, he began a kind of historical lecture rather than a speech. There was something engaging about it – all the more so since it ran counter to everything his opponents' propaganda had led one to expect: a hysterical demagogue, a shrieking, gesticulating fanatic in uniform. He did not allow the applause to tempt him from his sober tone. It seemed as if he were candidly presenting his anxieties about the future. His irony was softened by a somewhat self-conscious humour. His South German charm reminded Speer agreeably of his own native region – Speer was born in

Mannheim. Then the initial shyness would disappear; at times the pitch rose and Hitler would speak urgently and with hypnotic persuasiveness. Speer was carried away on the wave of enthusiasm that almost physically bore the speaker along from sentence to sentence. It swept away any scepticism, any reservations. Opponents were given no chance to speak. The citizens of the Third Reich listened spellbound and at the end the applause was shattering – frightening, even.

On Honour

IN A LETTER to Lord Rothermere on 3 May 1935 Hitler wrote, 'Since the [Great] War as an active politician, I have preached unswervingly the necessity of both nations [England and Germany] burying the hatchet for ever. I am convinced that such an understanding can only take place between honourable nations. I hold that there is no possibility of concluding agreements with a people without honour, and I regard such agreements as entirely worthless.' Hitler ruthlessly disregarded all the political agreements with most of the European countries and Russia.

Nuclear Research, Stage 1

WILLIAM SHIRER noticed the worsening state of German higher education in the 1930s. 'The great German universities now began to teach what they called *German* physics, *German* chemistry, *German* mathematics.' Hitler had a great respect for Professor Philipp Lenard of Heidelberg University, a Nobel Prize laureate in physics (1920). Lenard joined the Nazi Party in its early days and told Hitler that 'science, like every other human product, is racial and conditioned by blood'. He attacked Einstein and the Theory of Relativity, and persuaded Hitler that 'the Jew conspicuously lacks understanding for the truth . . . being in this respect in contrast to the Aryan research scientist with his careful and serious will to truth . . . Jewish physics is thus a phantom and a phenomenon of degeneration of fundamental German physics.' Professor Wilhelm Müller of Aachen Technical College and Professor Ludwig Bieberback of Berlin University were unanimous in their agreement: modern physics, and this included nuclear physics, was in reality a bid for 'Jewish world rule'. So to Hitler nuclear physics were 'Jewish physics'. Thus Alfred Rosenberg, later to be Minister of Education, took his cue from his master, and totally failed to support nuclear research.

'The Happiest Day of My Life'

THE ANGLO-GERMAN Naval Agreement was finally concluded by an exchange of notes on 18 June 1935. After the First World War the victorious Allies signed a series of treaties fixing the relative sizes of the British, American, Japanese, French and Italian navies in the ratio 5:5:3:1:1. Hitler had publicly declared his intention that the nascent German Navy should be built up to a strength of 35 per cent of the British Navy. Joachim von Ribbentrop, Erich Kordt, assistant to Konstantin von Neurath, the Foreign Minister, and Hitler's interpreter Paul Otto Schmidt, plus three German naval experts, took on the British Foreign Office and the British Admiralty. For two weeks the negotiations rumbled on. The German team won hands down. From his detached American viewpoint, Shirer wrote, 'The Wilhelmstrasse [German government] were elated. Germany gets a U-boat tonnage equal to that of Britain. German submarines almost beat them in the last war and may in the next.' It was undeniably a great victory for Hitler's foreign policy. Ribbentrop flew to join Hitler and Admiral Raeder in Hamburg. The Führer declared that the conclusion of the Agreement marked the happiest day of his life.

Emissaries to the Royal Family

HITLER KEPT UP a dialogue with the British royal family. Baron William de Ropp, from an aristocratic Baltic family, married an Englishwoman, was naturalized British and joined the Royal Flying Corps in the First World War, where he met Frederick Winterbotham (later a group captain in the RAF). In the late 1920s he moved to Berlin, became a political journalist and wrote for the London *Times*. He could pass as a German, a Russian, a Balt or an Englishman. De Ropp met Rosenberg, established himself in Nazi society and developed a personal relationship with Hitler. He became Hitler's chief agent of *rapprochement* between Germany and England's influential 'players' and was also a double agent. He brought peers, generals, an admiral and many journalists to Germany to meet Hitler, Hess and Rosenberg. In January 1935 de Ropp met the Duke of Kent who told him that Britain was reconciled to the rearmament plans of Hitler. He visited the Duke again in January 1936 supposedly 'at the request of King Edward VIII'. Rosenberg recorded in his diary, 'R. gave the Duke the benefit of his personal experience of many years.'

In 1936, however, Hitler deployed a cousin to the British royal family, Charles Edward (Carl Eduard), Duke of Saxe-Coburg and Gotha, and also Duke of Albany, being a grandson of Queen Victoria, a senior officer in the SA. On his visits to London he stayed at Kensington Palace, called on the new King Edward VIII at Fort Belvedere near Windsor, had tea with Queen Mary and attended a State dinner at Buckingham Palace. Saxe-Coburg asked the King whether a meeting between Hitler and the Prime Minister, Stanley Baldwin, might be considered, and reported to the Führer that the answer was, 'Who is king here, Baldwin or I? I myself wish to talk to Hitler and will do so here or in Germany. Tell him that, please.'

Hitler's Appearance – a Feminine Viewpoint

PRINCESS STEPHANIE VON HOHENLOHE, who developed a close acquaintanceship with the Nazi hierarchy – and was one of the links between Hitler's regime and Britain – left a vivid description Hitler from her meetings with him in the mid-1930s. She noted 'his light brown hair, not black at all, his oft-caricatured forelock, combed diagonally across his forehead,' but she did not like his nose, moustache, small mouth or coarse feet. His front teeth were edged with a thin gold strip, but his pale blue eyes were pleasant and, she said, might even be called beautiful except that they protruded slightly. His skin was very fine, almost translucent, always very pale with little pink spots on his cheeks. The Princess thought he was probably not healthy. She admired his artistic hands but noticed that he constantly scratched nervously with his thumbnail on the skin of his index finger so that it was always sore.

Operation Schulung and the King's Promise

THE LOCARNO PACT was a non-aggression treaty signed in 1925 between Germany, France and Belgium, guaranteed by Britain and Italy, which accepted the post-Versailles frontiers of the three countries and the permanent demilitarization of the Rhineland. Under Hitler's orders, in May 1935 General von Blomberg, the Minister of Defence and Commander-in-Chief of the Wehrmacht, planned the highly secret Operation Schulung to seize and reoccupy the demilitarized Rhineland – the 'surprise blow at lightning speed'. In February 1936 Hitler summoned Ribbentrop, his ambassador to Britain, Neurath and von Blomberg, now a field marshal, to a conference to discuss three options for the French-occupied Rhineland. Hitler preferred unilateral remilitarization by force – the third option. At once

Ribbentrop blurted out, 'The third, *mein Führer*, the third,' before the other two could give a view. Blomberg felt the Wehrmacht was not ready; Neurath thought that negotiation to reoccupy would succeed. But, as Himmler remarked to his masseur, Felix Kersten (who was later to claim credit for saving the lives of many Jews, through his closeness to Himmler), Ribbentrop had made himself indispensable by always seeming to be in agreement with his Führer. On Ribbentrop's advice Hitler chose a weekend to launch his coup. On 7 March 1936 the Wehrmacht, with only three battalions and horsedrawn transport, 'recovered' the frontier cities of Aachen, Trier and Saarbrücken. Neurath summoned the ambassadors of Britain, France, Belgium and Italy, the Locarno signatories, to his office in the Wilhelmstrasse, Berlin. He denounced the Locarno Pact – Hitler's first treaty, now broken. But the Führer almost immediately proposed to a hysterical audience of brown-shirted deputies of the Reichstag, his latest 'peace' plans, with five different proposals and pacts. Facing across the new frontier was the mighty blue-clad French army, which did nothing martial at all. Weak in morale and equipment, it was just a paper tiger. On the night of 7 March Albert Speer, Hitler's architect and friend, was part of the Führer's entourage travelling by train to Munich. At one station a message was handed to Hitler, who sighed with relief, 'At last! The King of England will not intervene. He is keeping his promise. That means it can all go well.'

A plebiscite at the end of March showed that 98 per cent of Germans approved of Hitler's coup in the Rhineland. The Führer took Ribbentrop and his wife on a special cruise on the Rhine to celebrate, and on 20 June Ribbentrop had a private audience with Edward VIII in London.

Approach to Churchill

WHEN RIBBENTROP ARRIVED in London in October 1936 he hoped to win useful friends in England through large-scale bribery. Hjalmar Schacht, the President of the Reichsbank, had produced a grant of 1 million Reichsmarks for this purpose. Ribbentrop's reports to Hitler of 29 October and 12 November 1935 (preparing for his mission of 1936) contained references to making a financial approach to Winston Churchill, no less. Ribbentrop did have a meeting with Churchill, who had no government post at the time – a rather stormy meeting. At one stage Hitler's emissary said, 'war is inevitable,' and Churchill replied, 'If you plunge us all into another Great War, we will bring the whole world against you, like last time.'

Tschapperl

EVA BRAUN was in charge of Hitler's private life and was his personal guest at the magnificent Berghof in Berchtesgaden, but Martin Bormann paid her allowance from Hitler, and all other household expenses. In front of the staff Hitler addressed her as 'Fraülein Braun', but in private he called her *'Tschapperl'*, which translates roughly as 'bumpkin', 'little idiot' or 'wench'. The jealous Nazi wives called her (though not to her face) *'die blöde Kuh'* ('silly cow'). By the beginning of 1936, however, her role was more clearly defined and Hitler instructed his staff and servants at the Berghof to call her *'Chefin'*, or *'gnädiges Fraülein'*, respectable forms of address, or *'Kindl'*, *'Patscherl'* or *'Schnacks'*, which are pet names for 'child'. After a number of years together Eva was allowed to call her lover Adolf or Adi, and to use the familiar 'du'. To everyone else after he became Chancellor he was addressed by the formal 'Sie' and known as der Führer, even by old 'friends' such as Göring.

Humorous Hitler

BEING A DICTATOR is a serious business – foes in front and foes behind – and his courtiers maintained that Hitler had no sense of humour and never laughed. At a Nuremberg rally William Shirer saw him laugh heartily at least a dozen times. 'He would rear back his head as he did so, the forelock of his dark brown hair, parted on the right side, would fall over his left temple to the eye until, still laughing, he would shake it back by a jerk of the head or the swish of his hand.'

Hitler's Lickspittle

RIBBENTROP had set up two 'friendship societies' in Berlin: the *Deutsch-Englische Gesellschaft*, linked to the Anglo-German Fellowship in England; and the *Deutsch-Französische Gesellschaft* linked to the Comité France-Allemagne in Paris. The *Dienststelle Ribbentrop* (his 'alternative' foreign ministry, in competition with the Foreign Minister, Neurath) was the key player in organizing fairly discreet Nazi propaganda. Personalities and delegations from both England and France visited Germany and often had the doubtful pleasure of an audience with Hitler. Banquets were given, periodicals were published, letters were written to newspapers. Ribbentrop also organized pressure groups to lobby for the return of the German colonies sequestrated in 1919, and also for a 'friendship' alliance with the Japanese Military Attaché in Berlin, Lieutenant-Colonel Oshima Hiroshi. Erich Kordt, who served Ribbentrop from 1934 to 1940 wrote, 'he endeavoured to anticipate Hitler's opinions and if anything to be in advance of Hitler along the path he might follow . . . when he had gained from Hitler's hangers-on what the Führer's course might be, he strongly came out in favour of that policy as his own. If Ribbentrop found that

Hitler had taken a stand different from what he had expected, he would immediately change his attitude.' And as Himmler noted, 'Ribbentrop was irreplaceable ... For Hitler trusted no one so much as him. No one could explain foreign policies to him so well. Ribbentrop's art of exposition was unique and entirely suited to Hitler's way of thought [that is, he agreed with Hitler].'

Hitler's Train

IN MID-1936 Hitler's own special train, rather strangely called 'Amerika', was completed. It consisted of a steam engine and fifteen Pullman carriages, protected at front and rear by banks of 2-cm quick-firing anti-aircraft guns mounted on flatcars, manned by a crew of twenty-six. Hitler's own Pullman, No. 10206, was in the centre, along with that of the press chief (Goebbels, who used it occasionally), a communications centre with a 700-watt shortwave radio transmitter, a kitchen and an ablutions carriage.

The Olympic Games of 1936

IN THE FIRST TWO WEEKS of August 1936, the XIth Modern Olympiad – 'Hitler's Olympics' – took place in Berlin. It was held in the biggest stadium in the world, designed by Albert Speer, Hitler's favourite architect, in an imposing classical style. The crowd numbered 110,000 and overhead the massive airship *Hindenburg* trailed the Olympic flag. Swastika banners wreathed the city of Berlin and Richard Strauss conducted a choir of 1,000 singing the national anthem 'Deutschland, Deutschland Über Alles', then the Nazi Party Anthem 'Horst Wessel Lied' and the new 'Olympic Hymn'. Extravaganzas were organized by Herman Göring and Joseph Goebbels. Although the German athletes won the most medals, the world remembers that Olympiad for the magnificent Jesse Owens, the black American runner who won *four* gold medals, and whose success infuriated Hitler and the Nazis. Hitler attended every day and it was a huge propaganda success for the Nazi regime with four million spectators attending, and over 3,000 radio programmes in 50 languages were broadcast round the world. Hitler was delighted because 'the young sportsmen of the Reich took thirty-three gold medals and the British, notwithstanding the advantages of their college system of education, were only able to win eight!'

'My Dear Princess'

PRINCESS STEPHANIE VON HOHENLOHE was for six years an influential go-between bearing Lord Rothermere's expensive gifts to the Führer, coming to know the entire Hitler coterie. Ribbentrop detested her and told Hitler that she was a 'full Jewess'; Goebbels's diary commented that 'the Princess is very pushy'; and Putzi warned Hitler to be very careful of her. But the Führer was taken with her and saw to it that the Gestapo should investigate her family tree and find it to be unexceptionable. Hitler wrote letters to her and made her a present of a signed photograph in a silver frame bearing the dedication 'In memory of a visit to Berchtesgaden.' His letters to Stephanie always started off 'My dear Princess'. During one tête-à-tête Hitler stroked her hair; another time he gave her an intimate pinch on the cheek. He also gave her a dog – which she never collected. In 1937 Hitler approved a presentation to her of a medal, the Honorary Cross of the German Red Cross, by its President, the Duke of Saxe-Coburg and Gotha. The next year, on 10 June, in the Reich Chancellery, she became a 'Bride of the National Socialist Workers' Party', the Führer himself pinning the Gold Medal of Honour to her bosom. His signature was engraved on its reverse. She was now a *de facto* Party member and an 'honorary Aryan'.

It all ended in tears. Hitler fired his adjutant, Wiedemann, for his liaison with the Princess, and Lord Rothermere's contract ended in January 1938. Rashly she sued him, lost, and fled to the USA with her German lover. While there she was most useful to the Office of Strategic Studies (forerunner of the CIA), providing insight into the Nazi dictator's character.

Hitler's 'Unshakeable Squire'

ON 30 OCTOBER 1936 the Propaganda Minister, Joseph Goebbels, celebrated his ten-year anniversary as Gauleiter of Berlin-Brandenburg. There were exhibitions and presents including a simple log cabin, and a midnight rally at which Hitler praised him as 'a faithful unshakeable squire of the Party . . . [who] had marched on ahead to Berlin, a fanatic filled with faith. Your name stands inscribed over this ten-year struggle of the National Socialist movement in Berlin!' Then, most unusual for Hitler, who avoided physical contact apart from handshakes, he thumped Goebbels awkwardly on the shoulder. No wonder Goebbels wrote in his diary, 'Hitler has honoured me as never before . . . How happy I am.'

Hitler's Best Horse

IN 1936 the Nazi Party radicals, Goebbels, Rosenberg, Himmler and Ley, plus Göring, doubted whether it was worth trying to secure the friendship of the British. The October Protocols signed on 23 October were hailed by Mussolini as the foundation of a new Rome-Berlin Axis. The Nazi radicals, in the aftermath of the Rhineland 'coup' and the huge, fairly secret rearmament plan, felt that Britain and France were on the sidelines. Hitler, however, sent Ribbentrop with a retinue of forty-four to London on 25 October. Hitler's parting words to his emissary were, 'Bring England into the Anti-Comintern Pact: that would fulfil my dearest wish. I have sent you to England as the best horse in my stable. See what you can do.'

The Abdication – the *Führerprinzip*

THE FÜHRER WAS BAFFLED and disappointed when King Edward VIII put his personal happiness before his royal duties and abdicated on 12 December 1936. Ambassador von Ribbentrop explained to Hitler that Stanley Baldwin's real motive in the abdication crisis had been to defeat those 'plotters' who had been working through Mrs Simpson and the King with the object of reversing present British policy and bringing about an Anglo-German entente. Hitler looked on 'the King as a man after his own heart and one who understood the *Führerprinzip* and was ready to introduce it into his country'. He thought Edward was the most intelligent prince he had ever met. Speer was told, 'I am certain that through him [Edward] permanent friendly relations with England could have been achieved. If he had stayed, everything would have been different. His abdication was a severe loss for us.'

The Messiah

HITLER, GÖRING AND HIMMLER, the leading members of the Nazi Party, were deeply steeped in magical and occult practices, as well as holding rather strange religious views. So too was Hess, while Bormann, Goebbels and Rosenberg had more than a sprinkling of occultism. Hitler had been presented to the country – by himself of course, but vehemently by Goebbels – as Germany's 'Messiah'. The Nazi rallies were carefully staged in a quasi-religious atmosphere, with no reproaches from the Christian churches. The Mayor of Hamburg stated, 'We can communicate directly to God through Adolf Hitler,' and in 1937 a group of German Christians claimed, 'Hitler's word is God's law.' The head of the Hitler Youth, Baldur von Schirach, said at the Nuremberg Trials after the war, 'The service of Germany appears to us to be genuine and sincere service of God: the banner of the Third Reich appears to us to be His banner and the Führer of the people is the saviour whom He sent to rescue us.' Hitler had given the nation back its pride, turned massive unemployment into full employment. He had smashed the feudal class system of the Weimar Republic. Hitler was indeed Germany's Messiah.

Baby Snatcher and Brainwasher

ON MAY DAY 1937 Hitler made a speech in Berlin that included a rare joke, about the deliberate brainwashing of the German youth. 'We have begun, above all, with the youth. There are old idiots out of whom nothing can be made any more' – pause for laughter – 'We take their children away from them. We bring them up to be a new kind of German. When a child is seven it does not yet have any feeling about its birth and origin. One child is like another. At that age we take them and form them into a community until they are eighteen. But we don't let them go then. They enter the party, the SA and SS and other formations, or they march directly into the factories, the Labour Front, the Labour Service and they go into the army for two years.' From 1933 onwards the whole of Germany, or anyway about 95 per cent, marched dutifully behind the Führer and his Third Reich.

Germany's Regained Honour

IN 1936 admiration for the Führer was widespread throughout Germany. Unemployment had been practically wiped out, living standards were undoubtedly improving and more consumer goods were available. The dance halls and cinemas were full, the

German Labour Front organized 'Strength through Joy' camps and cruise-ship voyages abroad. The *Volksempfänger* 'people's radio' was in three-quarters of German homes and by 1939 almost four million sets had been sold. In a mere three years Hitler had apparently rescued his country from the shame and misery of the Weimar 'democracy'. The loss of civil rights, repression of the Left, discrimination against the Jews and other unfortunates appeared to be a price worth paying. 'In those three years [1933–6], Germany has regained its honour, found belief again, and overcome its greatest economic distress.' Hitler also stated, 'We have no territorial claims to make in Europe.' In the 29 March 1936 election the Nazi Party (the only one standing) had a vote of 98.9 per cent backing Hitler.

The Windsor Visit

THE DUKE OF WINDSOR (as Edward VIII had become after his abdication) and his new wife made a two-week visit to Germany in October 1937, ostensibly to study housing and working conditions. They were entertained by the Görings, visited Essen where the Krupp steelworks were very busy producing armaments (which they'd been banned from doing by the Treaty of Versailles), Leipzig, and Dresden, where the Duke of Saxe-Coburg and Gotha gave a dinner party for them and the Duchess was addressed as 'Your Royal Highness', while the Duke of Windsor gave numerous Nazi salutes. They also visited Nuremberg and Stuttgart and on 22 October took tea with the Führer at Berchtesgaden. Hitler said to Schmidt, his interpreter, 'She would have made a good queen.' The Duchess wrote later, 'I could not take my eyes off Hitler' – she admired his long, slim hands and 'felt the impact of a great inner force'. His eyes were 'truly extraordinary – intense, unblinking, magnetic, burning with . . . peculiar fire.' In August 1939 the Duke and Hitler exchanged telegrams. Hitler recalled later, in 1942: 'The real reason for the destruction of the Duke of Windsor was, I am sure, his speech at the old veterans' rally in Berlin, at which he declared that it would be the task of his life to effect a reconciliation between Britain and Germany. That rally in Berlin bore the stamp of sincere and mutual esteem, and the subsequent treatment of the Duke of Windsor was an evil omen; to topple over so fine a pillar of strength was both wicked and foolish.'

The Reluctant Butcher's Dogs

COLONEL FRIEDRICH HOSSBACH, Hitler's Wehrmacht adjutant, took the minutes of a top-level meeting chaired by the Führer in the Chancellery on 6 November 1937. Werner von Blomberg, Minister of Defence, Admiral Raeder, Commander-in-Chief of the Navy, Hermann Göring, Commander-in-Chief of the Luftwaffe, Werner von Fritsch, Commander-in-Chief of the Army, and Konstantin von Neurath, the Foreign Minister, attended. The meeting was called to discuss and agree a rearmament programme (yet another) and the allocation of materials and arms between the three services. Hitler instead delivered a four-hour monologue on the need for *Lebensraum* and how this was to be won. 'Germany's problem could only be solved by means of force . . . the extra space would have to be in Europe but there were two hate-inspired antagonists, Britain and France, to whom a German colossus in the centre of Europe was a thorn in the flesh.' Germany's military might would reach its peak by 1943–4, after which the other powers would catch up. The first moves would be the annexation of Austria and Czechoslovakia, which would secure the eastern and southern flanks. Hitler thought that Britain and France had already tacitly written off Czechoslovakia and would not interfere. His broad plan was in *Mein Kampf*, but nevertheless the generals were 'shaken to the core'. 'Generals should be like a butcher's dog who has to be held fast by the collar because otherwise he threatens to attack anyone in sight.' Hitler was contemptuous of Blomberg and Fritsch and the next year the SS framed both of them for sexual misdemeanours – probably with help from Göring. Both were forced to resign and Hitler put his own choices in their places.

In the history books the meeting was called the 'Hossbach Memorandum'.

'The Hitler Nobody Knows'

HEINRICH HOFFMANN, Hitler's friend and a talented photographer, travelled everywhere with Hitler as his official photographer (an album of his 'court' photographs is housed in the Imperial War Museum in London). In 1937 his book *Hitler, Ihn Keiner Kennt* (*The Hitler Nobody Knows*), first published in 1933, had to be reissued, with diplomatic changes. Photographs of the Nazi leader being friendly with Ernst Röhm, whom he had just had killed, were not appropriate, so Hitler chose new photographs for Hoffmann's opus. Now he would be shown as a good-natured, casual, private individual in leather shorts, or rowing a boat, picnicking in the meadows, walking in the Bavarian woods, surrounded by children or youngsters, in artists' studios. But always friendly, relaxed, accessible – and harmless. The book proved to be Hoffmann's greatest success.

Blood

HITLER PIONEERED a rather sinister technique – using allusions to or images of blood to evoke deep-rooted elemental feelings in his Teutonic audiences. For instance, the 'Night of the Long Knives' was often referred to as the 'blood purge'. Racial inter-marriage between German Aryans and Jews was described as

Blutschande or 'blood shame'. In the SS mythology promoted by Himmler, the phrase *'Blut und Boden'* ('blood and earth') was used to express the primitive relationship between the peasantry and the earth. Hitler was very keen on pageantry, and flags and standards were particularly important to him. *Die Blutfahne,* the 'blood flag' was a flag made sacrosanct by the very few martyrs of the abortive 1923 Munich putsch. He also devised many decorations, orders and medals for his Nazi Party, including *der Blutorden,* 'the blood order', a prestigious decoration for the faithful few.

'Simplicity Makes a Striking Effect'

ON 13 MARCH 1938 German troops marched into Austria. Hitler sent for a map of Central Europe and showed his cronies how 'Czechoslovakia was now caught in pincers'. He also said he would 'remain eternally grateful to the Duce' who had given his consent to the invasion of Austria. His Italian journey in May 1938 was made in order to show Mussolini and King Victor Emmanuel III his gratitude and also to view the art treasures of Rome and Florence. Resplendent uniforms were designed for the German entourage to match the pomp and ceremony of the Italian courtiers. Hitler loved this pomp but his own dress was always modest – a matter of careful strategy. 'My surroundings must look magnificent. Then my simplicity makes a striking effect.'

Hitler's Spring Clean

ON SATURDAY, 5 February 1938 Hitler, in another astonishing 'coup', smashed the German Army High Command, which he suspected might not carry out his orders for the campaigns he had secretly planned. Having cashiered the two men who had built up the German Army from scratch: Field Marshal Werner von Blomberg, Minister of War and Commander-in-Chief of the

Armed Forces; and General von Fritsch, Commander-in-Chief of the Wehrmacht, Hitler then made himself Supreme Commander of the Armed Forces, relieved sixteen senior generals of their commands and transferred forty-four others. Three key diplomats were fired or replaced: the ambassadors in Rome, Tokyo and Vienna, plus the old financial wizard Dr Schacht, who had kept Nazi Germany solvent. A thorough and, for some, worrying 'spring clean'.

'The Game of Danger'

'You cannot understand what it is to live in a dictatorship: you can't understand the game of danger but above all you cannot understand the fear on which the whole thing is based. Nor I suppose have you any concept of the charisma of a man such as Hitler.' For twelve years, from the age of twenty-nine, the keenly intelligent Albert Speer was Hitler's personal architect and worked closely with him. Speer's friend and colleague Karl Hettlage told Speer in the summer of 1938, 'You are Hitler's unhappy love,' to which Speer later wrote in answer: 'And you know what I felt? Happy, joyful.'

Nervous Breakdown

WILLIAM SHIRER saw Hitler in the garden of the Dreesen Hotel, Godesberg, on 22 September 1938, and described him as walking in a ladylike way with dainty little steps. He cocked his right shoulder nervously after every few steps and his left leg snapped up at the same time in a nervous tic. He had ugly black patches under his eyes and he seemed on the edge of a nervous breakdown. Hitler was preparing to have a top-level meeting with Neville Chamberlain, the British Prime Minister, and was rehearsing to himself what his demands were going to be.

'Hitler's Terrific Victory'

IN MUNICH, on 30 September 1938, it was game, set and match to Hitler and his team – Göring, Ribbentrop, Goebbels, Hess and General Wilhelm Keitel, Chief of Staff of the Armed Forces (OKW). They swaggered out of the Führerhaus at 2 a.m. after Hitler and Mussolini had beaten a submissive Neville Chamberlain and a totally broken Édouard Daladier. Daladier, the French Prime Minister, was reputed to be afraid to return to Paris in case he was attacked by a hostile mob. He had sacrificed France's position and lost her main prop in Eastern Europe. A disastrous day for France. At 1.30 a.m. Chamberlain and Daladier had told Dr Mastny, the Czech Minister in Berlin, and Dr Masaryk of the Prague Foreign Office that Czechoslovakia would have to accept defeat and surrender the Sudetenland. Chamberlain saw Hitler the following morning and cobbled together a 'spin' so that he could boast from No. 10 Downing Street. 'Peace with honour. I believe it is peace for our time.' The gullible British public sang 'For He's A Jolly Good Fellow'. Winston Churchill was one of the few who read the situation right: 'We have sustained a total, unmitigated defeat . . . all the countries of Mittel Europa and the Danube valley, one after the other will be drawn into the vast system of Nazi politics . . .' All the German papers said the same thing: 'Hitler's terrific victory over Britain and France'.

The Carpet-Chewer

THE JOURNALISTS covering the machinations of Germany over the Sudetenland, Czechoslovakia and Austria in the 1930s kept talking among themselves about Hitler the '*teppichfresser*'. When the Führer was suffering his worst nervous crises in private his behaviour would often take a bizarre form. Throwing a tantrum and screaming in fury or frustration about Edvard Beneš, the Czech president, or anybody else who had crossed him, he would fling himself onto the floor and chew the edge of the carpet. Hence *teppichfresser*, the 'carpet chewer'.

The Scrap of Paper

CASE GREEN was Hitler's plan for the invasion and conquest of Czechoslovakia, planned for 1 October 1938. The British government learned of this in August, so the Cabinet met on the 30th and agreed to put pressure on the Czechs to give in to Hitler. Border incidents were staged by German troops and in conference on 2 September Hitler declared in ringing tones '*Es lebe der Krieg*', 'Long live war' – adding 'even if it lasts from two to eight years.' President Beneš accepted London's view and conceded most of Hitler's demands. The French, who had a treaty with Czechoslovakia, suffered a collective collapse of nerve. Neville Chamberlain, the British Prime Minister, went to Godesberg to visit Hitler, who, like Oliver Twist, made more demands. Eventually the Munich Agreement was signed on 24 September and Hitler had the Czechoslovak Sudeten territory ceded to the Third Reich. Chamberlain, having sold out the Czechs, flew back to London in triumph declaring he had obtained 'peace for our time'. Hitler and Ribbentrop were cheated of the war they desired and Hitler assured the latter, 'Don't take it all so seriously. That scrap of paper is of no significance whatever.' In March 1939 – the next spring – Hitler's troops marched unopposed into the remainder of Czechoslovakia.

Kristallnacht

THIS SINGLE terrifying action on the night of 9–10 November 1938 opened the eyes of the world to the realities of the Nazi regime. Herschel Grynszpan, a German Jewish refugee in Paris, murdered a German Legation secretary, Ernst von Rath, although Rath was totally opposed to Nazism. With Hitler's express approval, Reinhard Heydrich, Chief of the Reich Security head office, organized the pogrom having been advised by Goebbels that 'spontaneous' anti-Jewish riots would not be discouraged. Heydrich sent urgent orders to all police HQ for 'spontaneous' riots across Germany. As a result, 191 synagogues were set on fire, 815 Jewish shops and 171 Jewish homes were destroyed, 74 Jews were killed and no fewer than 20,000 arrested. Damage costing 25 million marks was caused including 5 million for broken glass windows – hence the name of the purge. Germany's 600,000 Jews were collectively fined 1 billion marks and many Jewish businesses and properties were confiscated. The process of Aryanization had begun. The US Ambassador to Germany was recalled and on 14 November Roosevelt made a speech condemning *Kristallnacht*. Jewish emigration swelled to a torrent. Public opinion in Britain was horrified, although the appeasers continued their pathetic efforts.

Rousseau, Mirabeau, Robespierre and Napoleon

HUGH TREVOR-ROPER, the brilliant 'Hitler watcher', wrote of Adolf Hitler, 'He was the Rousseau, the Mirabeau, the Robespierre and the Napoleon of his revolution [the creation of the Third Reich]; he was its Marx, its Lenin, its Trotsky and its Stalin. By character and nature he may have been far inferior to most of these but he nevertheless managed to achieve what all of them could not: he dominated his revolution in every phase, even in the moment of defeat. That argues a considerable understanding of the forces he evoked!'

Assassination Attempts Against Hitler

THERE WERE a number of attempts on Hitler's life – all doomed to failure. Among them, on 9 November 1938 Maurice Bavaud, a Swiss waiter, stalked Hitler with a gun in the Bürgerbräukeller inn, Munich and on the Obersalz mountain. After a secret trial by the People's Court, he was tried, sentenced and beheaded.

Another attempt was made by George Elser, a thirty-six-year-old Swabian watchmaker who, in November 1939, constructed a time bomb and placed it in a pillar in the huge Bürgerbräukeller in Munich. It exploded eleven minutes after Hitler had left to catch a train for Berlin, killing eight of his faithful supporters and wounding many others.

Count Claus Graf von Stauffenberg placed a bomb (in a brief-case) under a table at an important conference at Obersalzberg on 20 July 1944. He was part of a substantial conspiracy to kill Hitler – but although four men were killed, Hitler was only slightly injured. Von Stauffenberg was caught and executed, as were many others.

Hitler Mutti

MANY WOMEN, including middle-aged ladies, fell under Hitler's spell. In 1938 the women attending his meetings responded even more enthusiastically and generously than the men. Some of these devoted females were of the 'hysterical type, who found an emotional ecstasy in surrender to the man on the platform. He could twitch their very nerves with his forcefulness.' Most of these women, however, were as intelligently interested as the men and without their financial aid the early years of the Party would have been much more difficult.

Many of them looked upon Hitler as a favourite son and they became known as 'Hitler mutti', Hitler mothers. His very

✠ ─── ✠

wealthy patroness, Frau Hélène Bechstein, and Frau Elizabeth Büchner, a towering Brunhild type, both gave him rhinoceros-hide dog whips. This might have become a personal tradition, dating from the time an elderly widow, Carola Hoffmann, whom he used to visit regularly, asked him what she could give him as a present. He apparently suggested a rhinoceros-hide dog whip – like the one Alois used to beat him with. Perhaps owning a whip of this kind was a way of cocking a snook at his late father, and of confronting his early frustrations.

'Operation Case White'

HITLER HAD PREPARED very carefully for the invasion and conquest of Poland, and 'Case White' was the code name for the military operation. 'Operation Himmler' was the code name for the SD (*Sicherheitsdienst*) under Reinhard Heydrich, Himmler's SS deputy, who would simulate fake Polish aggression in the Danzig corridor by seizing the Gleiwitz radio station. 'Operation Canned Goods' was a revolting plan using condemned men from concentration camps dressed in Polish uniforms, killing them by lethal injection and placing their bodies for the Nazi photographers as Polish 'saboteurs' – evidence of Polish 'aggression'. Hitler and Ribbentrop desperately wanted a non-aggression pact with Stalin via Molotov, his Foreign Minister. The Russians, worried about Japanese military activities on their eastern borders, were relatively happy to sign a vast trade agreement *and* a non-aggression pact with Germany. Hitler's *der Tag* for Case White was 4.30 a.m. on 26 August 1939. As the countdown for total war approached both he and Ribbentrop were hysterical and close to nervous breakdown. Moreover, England and France, which had detected many signs of the impending invasion of Poland, had to be kept reassured about Germany's peaceful intentions. Finally, Hitler could bear

'WHY SO STARTLED, FÜHRER? DON'T YOU RECOGNIZE ONE OF YOUR
FIRST MEMBERS OF THE PARTY?'

the suspense no longer and sent a personal telegram to Stalin. Ribbentrop flew to Moscow, and eventually, on 24 August, the secret non-aggression pact between the Soviet Union and Germany was signed. Hitler was ecstatic. Breaking with his no-alcohol tradition, he had a few sips of champagne and exclaimed, 'Now Europe is mine – the others can have Asia. The world is in my pocket.' Hitler's armies launched their blitzkrieg ('lightning war') against Poland on 1 September.

'Fraülein Braun and My Dog'

BEFORE THE SECOND WORLD WAR Hitler talked to his closest friends of the time when, his political goals accomplished, he would withdraw from running the nation and retire to live in Linz. He would not interfere with affairs of state and people would turn to his successor quickly enough. Then he himself would be quickly forgotten. 'Perhaps one of my former associates will visit me occasionally. But I don't count on it. Aside from Fraülein Braun, I'll take no one with me. Fraülein Braun and my dog. I'll be lonely. Nobody will take any notice of me any more. They'll all go running after my successor. Perhaps once a year they'll show up for my birthday.'

Hitler's Secret Bank Account

IN THE FILE FO371/23083 in the British National Archives, Kew, is a letter received at the Foreign Office on 25 March 1939, index number C3982. It was written by Neville Bland of the British Legation in The Hague to Sir William Strang at the FO. 'My dear William, You may be interested to know that the father of the Commercial Secretary's Dutch clerk who is employed in the local Tax Collector's Office has informed Laming that there is an account with the Netherland Postal Cheque and Clearance

Service in the name of Eber Nachfolger GmbH, Thierstrasse 11, 22, Munich, Giro number 211846 and that, according to an Inspector of Taxes who in the course of his investigations discovered the fact, this account belongs to Herr Hitler.'

Almost certainly Max Amann was squirrelling away Hitler's substantial profits from the Eher Verlag publishing house into Holland. Probably *Mein Kampf* royalties were banked there, too.

Hitler's Terrible Stew

ON 31 MARCH 1939 Neville Chamberlain, 'looking gaunt and ill' (according to Harold Nicolson's *Diaries and Letters*) read out a statement to the House of Commons guaranteeing support for Poland's independence. When the news broke in Hitler's Reich Chancellery in Berlin, the Führer fell into a hideous rage: 'With features distorted by fury, he stormed up and down his room, pounded his fists on the marble table-top and spewed forth a series of savage imprecations. His eyes flashed with an uncanny light,' according to Admiral Wilhelm Canaris, head of the German military intelligence service (the *Abwehr*). 'He then growled this threat, "I'll cook them a stew that they'll choke on."' In 1934 Hitler had signed a ten-year non-aggression pact with Poland. In September 1939 on the pretext of annexing Gdańsk, Hitler's armies and those of Soviet Russia invaded Poland, which despite heroic defence was swiftly overwhelmed.

Count Ciano's Diary and the 'Pact of Steel'

COUNT GALEAZZO CIANO, the Italian Foreign Minister, who was married to Benito Mussolini's daughter, Edda, wrote in his diary on 28 April 1939: 'The Führer has delivered his speech in Berlin. It lasted exactly two hours and twenty minutes; it cannot be said that brevity is Hitler's most noticeable characteristic. Generally speaking the speech is less bellicose than one might have supposed on the information coming to us. The first reactions to the speech in the different capitals are also rather mild. Every word which leaves any hope of peaceful intention is received by the whole of humanity with immeasurable joy. No nation wants war today: the most that one can say is that they know war is inevitable . . .'

Hitler's speech demanded that Poland hand the city of Gdańsk over to Germany. He also revoked Germany's non-aggression pact with Poland and rejected US President Franklin D. Roosevelt's offer of mediation.

On 21 May Ciano arrived in Berlin for the formal signature of the 'Pact of Steel', which linked Mussolini's Fascist Italy with Hitler's Nazi Germany. Their 'united forces will act side by side for the securing of their living space and the maintenance of peace.' Of course, neither dictator had the faintest intention of keeping the peace.

'We Must Burn Our Boats'

HITLER FORBADE any minutes of confidential meetings, but a General of the Wehrmacht, Lieutenant-Colonel Rudolf Schmundt, did take notes at such a meeting held on 23 May 1939 in the Chancellery, which were found after the war was over. To his top military leaders, Göring, Generals Beck, Keitel and Walther von Brauchitsch, Admiral Raeder, plus Ribbentrop and Neurath, Hitler made it clear that there should be an 'attack on Poland at the first suitable moment . . . then the fight must be primarily against England and France. . . . Therefore England is our enemy and the showdown with England is a matter of life and death.' Holland and Belgium would have to be overrun. Their declarations of neutrality would be ignored. He was confident of defeating France, and the bases on that country's west coast would enable the Luftwaffe and U-boats to effect the blockade that would bring Britain to its knees. 'We must then burn our boats' – and a war of ten to fifteen years might be necessary.

The Death Knell of the British Empire

ON THE NIGHT OF 21 AUGUST 1939, while he was at supper, a note was handed to Hitler, who flushed deeply, then banged on the table so hard that the glasses rattled, and exclaimed in an excited voice, 'I have them! I have them!' Speer recalled that no one dared to ask any questions and the meal continued. At the end of it Hitler told his entourage, 'We are going to conclude a non-aggression pact with Russia. Here, read this. A telegram from Stalin.' A secret protocol, not for publication, was appended to the Non-Aggression Treaty whereby Stalin and Hitler agreed to divide Eastern Europe into spheres of influence: Finland, Estonia and Latvia to Russia, and Lithuania to Germany, while Poland would be partitioned along the rivers Narev, Vistula and San.

Goebbels held an evening press conference two days later; when Hitler wanted to know how the foreign correspondents had reacted, his propaganda chief answered, 'The sensation was fantastic. And when the church bells simultaneously began ringing outside, a British correspondent fatalistically remarked, "That is the death knell of the British Empire."' Hitler's euphoria knew no bounds. He was beyond the reach of fate.

'Hero of Ancient Myth'

AFTER THE NAZI–SOVIET PACT was signed in Moscow the Hitler coterie was divided into two camps. The Propaganda Minister, Goebbels, spoke openly and anxiously about the danger of war, considering the risks excessively high. Rather surprisingly, Hermann Göring, the most martial of the Hitler clique, recommended a peaceful line. The warmongers were Wilhelm Keitel, Chief of Staff of the Armed Forces (OKW) and Ribbentrop. Speer commented, 'In those days he [Hitler] seemed to me like a hero of ancient myth, conscious of his strength [who] could masterfully meet the test of the wildest undertakings.'

Hitler's view was that because of Germany's rapid rearmament it held a four-to-one advantage in strength . . . 'We have new weapons in all fields, the other side obsolete types.' The 'other side' Hitler had in mind was, of course, Poland. Not even Mussolini's inability to keep his alliance obligations could put off Hitler's launch of Operation Case White.

Chamberlain – the 'Schweinehund'

THE DAY AFTER the Non-Aggression Treaty was signed with Russia, Hitler briefed all his top military chiefs before the assault on Poland. General Franz Halder and Admiral Bohm recounted Hitler's speech: 'Essentially all depends on me, on my existence, because of my political talents . . . no one will ever again have the confidence of the whole German people as I have . . . No one knows how long I shall live. Therefore a showdown had better take place now . . . A life-and-death struggle. The destruction of Poland has priority. A quick decision, in view of the season . . . Close your hearts to pity! Act brutally! Eighty million people must obtain what is their right. Be hard and remorseless. Be steeled against all signs of compassion.' The only thing that worried Hitler was that Neville Chamberlain might pull another Munich on him. 'I am only afraid that some *Schweinehund* will make a proposal for mediation.'

'Destruction and Barbarism the Real Victors'

FRANCE'S PREMIER Édouard Daladier exchanged letters with Hitler in the last desperate days of August 1939. Hitler had already warned the people that the political situation was very grave. A week earlier, on 21 August, the incredible volte-face of the Russian-German pact was announced almost simultaneously with Hitler's arrogant demands to Poland. Daladier wrote a noble letter to the German leader asking Hitler to hold back from war, saying that there is no question that cannot be solved peacefully and reminding him that Poland was a sovereign nation. Daladier claimed that France would honour its obligations to Poland. Hitler regretted that France intended to fight to 'maintain a wrong' and said that Gdańsk and the Polish Corridor must be returned to Germany and that he realized full well the consequences of war. In his final letter, Daladier wrote, 'If French and German blood is now to be spilled, as it was twenty-five years ago . . . then each of the two peoples will fight confident of its own victory. But surely Destruction and Barbarism will be the real victors.'

The Chicago Gangsters

ON 19 SEPTEMBER 1939, in the Gdańsk Guild Hall, a gothic building of great beauty, Hitler made a conqueror's speech and ranted and roared, with carefully orchestrated effect and 'hysterical rage', mainly against Britain with which Germany was now at war. A group of international journalists had been invited to the Guild Hall to hear the Führer, among whom was William Shirer. When Hitler, Himmler, Brückner, Keitel and others passed him, all in dusty field grey, he noted that they were unshaven and looked like a pack of Chicago gangsters.

Unity Mitford's Near-Suicide Expenses

AFTER UNITY MITFORD'S NEAR-SUICIDE, Hitler personally guaranteed to pay for her treatment. Account No. 4415 at the Bayerische Gemeindebank in the name of Unity Mitford received on 1 November 1939 various payments from Hitler. Professor Magnus of the Chirurgische Universitatsklinik received over 3,000 marks. A further 1,300 Reichmarks were needed for hospital treatment and X-rays from Dr Albert Kohler. Unity had a private room in the clinic with a nurse in constant attendance. Hitler also paid for her repatriation to England. It was a sad ending to their strange relationship.

Stalin's Amusement

A FEW DAYS AFTER the double event of the 8 November 1939 bomb attack in the Munich Bürgerbräukeller and the entrapment of British agents in the 'Venlo Incident', Hitler, Himmler, Heydrich and Colonel Walter Schellenberg were dining together. The latter was asked for his views and replied, 'Great Britain will fight this war with all the fury and tenacity of which she has given proof in all wars in which she was thoroughly engaged.' Even if Germany occupied England the government would conduct the war from Canada. 'It will be a life-and-death struggle between countries of the same stock – and Stalin will look on with interest and amusement.'

'Bloodless Victories Demoralizing'

AFTER POLAND WAS OVERRUN in late 1939 Hitler frequently expressed this view: 'Do you think it would have been good fortune for our troops if we had taken Poland without a fight after obtaining Austria and Czechoslovakia without fighting?

'STEPPING STONES TO GLORY'

Believe me, not even the best army can stand that sort of thing. Victories without loss of blood are demoralizing. Therefore it was not only fortunate there was no compromise: at the time we would have had to regard it as harmful and I therefore would have struck in any case.'

Messrs HHHH

CHURCHILL BELIEVED that Hitler's almost feverish efforts to secure some kind of peace treaty with Britain meant that his overall war strategy was 'ripe for exploitation'. One of Churchill's oldest friends was Rex Leeper, head of Special Operations 1 (SO1), part of the new Special Operations Executive (SOE). Leeper's unit was based at Woburn Abbey in Bedfordshire, and specialized in political warfare. Leeper, Leonard Ingrams and Richard Crossman devised a 'Black Propaganda' scheme to fool Hitler, coded 'Messrs HHHH', which stood for Hitler, Hess, and Karl and Albrecht Haushofer, two of Hitler's geopolitical advisors. It would be a 'sting' to upset, disturb and possibly wreck Hitler's strategic plans. The plan was to encourage the Germans to attack Russia by misleading Hitler, hinting that many politicians in Britain and the USA preferred to see the overthrow of Russian Communism than of the German regime. A compromise peace between Britain and Germany would combine to destroy the *common* enemy, Communism. Churchill knew that, as part of the Nazi–Soviet Pact, Stalin was supplying Hitler with oil, petrol, food, munitions and machine parts – all the sinews of war – to work for Britain's destruction. Stalin's Russia in 1940 was a staunch German ally and it is probable that Messrs HHHH helped persuade Hitler that he should proceed with his secret plans (Operation Barbarossa) to invade the Soviet Union.

Anti-Semitism in the Inner Circle

FOR ALMOST ALL HIS LIFE Hitler was tormented by the thought of his (possibly) Jewish blood. But most of his repulsive henchmen were in the same boat. Himmler had Jewish relatives; Rosenberg had a Jewish mistress and almost certainly Jewish ancestors. Reinhard Heydrich, chairman of the Wannsee ('the Final Solution') Committee in January 1942, might have had a Jewish grandfather. Goebbels was once engaged to a Jewish girl and was nicknamed 'the Rabbi' by his staff. Adolf Eichmann (1900–62), who was set up by Himmler as head of the Central Office for Jewish Emigration in Vienna, was as a boy frequently taunted for his Semitic looks and Semitic family background. Karl Haushofer had a Jewish wife; Hitler's occult advisor Erik Jan Hanussen was Jewish; Luftwaffe General Erhard Milch's father was Jewish. Göring, Hess and Speer were the only prototype Aryans in the Hitler court. Himmler, Heydrich and Goebbels were the most rabid persecutors of the Jewish race in the Third Reich and seemed to vie with each other in their frenzied attacks.

Happy Christmas 'Cemented by Blood'

HITLER AND RIBBENTROP wired their Christmas greetings to Comrade Josef Stalin in Moscow on 21 December 1939. 'Best wishes for your personal well-being as well as for the prosperous future of the peoples of the friendly Soviet Union.' To which Stalin replied, 'The friendship of the peoples of Germany and the Soviet Union, cemented by blood, has every reason to be lasting and firm.' Eighteen months later, in Operation Barbarossa, the temporary alliance certainly was 'cemented by blood' as millions of soldiers and Russian civilians were slaughtered. As Poland was being devastated by Germany and Russia at the end of 1939, Shirer wrote, 'And now darkness. A new world. Black-out, bombs, slaughter, Nazism. Now the night and the shrieks of barbarism.'

Hitler's Avalanche

IN 1940 Hitler said to Himmler, Heydrich and Schellenberg, 'At the beginning I wanted to collaborate with Great Britain. But she rejected my advances . . . our real enemies, to the east, wait tranquilly for Europe to be exhausted . . . Churchill must understand that Germany also has the right to live . . . And I shall fight England till she gets off her pedestal. The day will come when she will show herself disposed to envisage an accord between us.' The young, tough SS Colonel Schellenberg questioned his Führer, 'But a war like this is comparable to an avalanche. And who would venture to plot the course of an avalanche?' 'My dear boy,' replied Hitler, 'those are my worries, leave them to me.'

Weser Exercise

HITLER'S SKILFUL OPERATION to seize Denmark and Norway, codename *Weserübung* ('Weser Exercise', after Germany's River Weser), depended on the German Navy seizing possession of the harbours, particularly in Norway, to give German naval forces direct access to the Atlantic and assure the flow of iron ore from neutral Sweden. On 8 April 1940, in the garden of the Chancellery, Hitler told Goebbels about the Weser Exercise, involving 250,000 men. Curiously, the Führer mentioned that the Norway operation was the *only* assignment he would give the navy – implying that a successful landing in England was hardly possible. Therefore Goebbels was told to maintain the public hatred of Britain at the previous level and not create expectations of an invasion of that country. On 16 July Hitler had half-heartedly given instructions for Operation Sealion, a landing operation on the English South Coast. In his diary, Goebbels noted in Hitler a certain 'fear of the water'.

The British Toehold

THE NORWEGIAN CAMPAIGN, described by Hitler as 'the cheekiest operation in modern history', had been brilliantly planned by his commanders Keitel, Alfred Jodl and Raeder. Troop transports were disguised as coal steamers, with heavy equipment, artillery, ammunition and provisions concealed below the coal. Fast German warships under cover of British flags would land troops at Trondheim, Stavanger and Narvik. Two battleships and ten destroyers guarded more troopships, and the treacherous fascist Norwegian politician Major Vidkun Quisling waited to form a German-controlled government. Paratroops landed and Oslo soon surrendered. But the Royal Navy sank half the German ships and two British troop landings at Namsos and Harstad brought Hitler to the verge of a nervous breakdown. In a panic he ordered the Luftwaffe to destroy Namsos and Åandalsnes and told his adjutants, 'I know the British. I came up against them in the Great War. Where they once get a toehold there is no throwing them out again.'

Annihilating Britain

HITLER, GOEBBELS AND SPEER were sitting in Hitler's Berlin salon in autumn 1939 watching a film of the Luftwaffe's Stuka dive bombers destroying Warsaw. Hitler was fascinated. The film ended with a montage of a plane diving towards the outlines of the British Isles. A burst of flame followed and the islands flew into the air in tatters. Hitler's enthusiasm was unbounded. 'That is what will happen to them! . . . That is how we will annihilate them!'

De Gaulle's Help

IN 1925, when Hitler was writing *Mein Kampf*, he detailed his plan to invade France through the Low Countries. This was confirmed in the secret Hossbach Memorandum of 1937. By 1940 the war was having an effect on the economic front in Germany and there was severe rationing, which was unpopular, although supplies from Russia, Austria and Denmark were helping. Germany badly needed the prosperous treasure troves of the Low Countries and France. Hitler planned *Fall Gelb* ('Operation Yellow') – the invasion of the Netherlands and Belgium – brilliantly. On 10 May 1940 the blitzkrieg started under Luftwaffe bombing of cities, Stukas divebombing resistance points and paratroopers dropping on fortresses and strongpoints. Panzers thrust through Dutch, Belgian, French and British defences and the 'fifth column' of saboteurs was in action. It was horrible but savagely effective. 'The hour of the decisive battle for the future of the German nation has come. The battle for the future of the German nation has come. The battle beginning today will decide the future of the German nation for the next thousand years,' Hitler promised on radio. Rotterdam was pulverized and Hitler threatened to do the same to Utrecht, Amsterdam and Paris. The French Maginot Line defences were bypassed and the *poilus* surrendered in their thousands. The German radio military communiqué called it 'a French rout'. Hitler refused to allow publication of casualty lists and every victory broadcast ended with the marching song: 'We march against England, Today we own Germany, Tomorrow the whole world.' Hitler claimed total credit for the success of *Fall Gelb*, 'I have again and again read Colonel de Gaulle's book on methods of modern warfare employing fully motorized units. I have learned a great deal from it.'

'Hitler Rages and Screams' and the Dunkirk Evacuation

THE WEHRMACHT, Luftwaffe, parachute and glider troops preceded by ten Panzer divisions had in Operation Yellow swept through the Low Countries and northern France, starting on 10 May 1940. Hitler had personally conceived the brilliant airborne drops that had captured vital bridges and Belgium's Eben Emael fortress. With its troops over the River Meuse by 13 May, the German High Command became alarmed at the success of General Ewald von Kleist's Panzer army. His Chief of Staff, General Franz Halder, kept a diary. '18 May. Every hour is precious, Führer HQ sees it differently. The Führer unaccountably keeps worrying about the south flank. He rages and screams that we are on the way to best ruin the whole campaign and that we are leading up to a defeat. He won't have any part of continuing the operation in a westward direction [towards Dunkirk].' On 21 May a British tank counter-attack near Arras caused alarm in the German Fourth Army. Hitler visited General von Rundstedt's HQ at Charleville on 24 May. General Blumentritt, a key officer at the meeting, told Liddell Hart, the British military historian 'Hitler was in a very good humour. He admitted that the course of the campaign had been "a decided miracle" and gave us his opinion that the war would be finished in six weeks . . . He then astonished us by speaking with admiration of the British Empire, of the necessity for its existence, and of the civilization that Britain had brought into the world . . . He concluded by saying that his aim was to make peace with Britain on a basis that she would regard as compatible with her honour to accept.' Von Rundstedt and General von Brauchitsch recommended that the terrain around Dunkirk was unsuitable for the German panzers, which were needed for a further attack to the south. Moreover, Göring had persuaded Hitler that the

Luftwaffe would finish off the encircled British and French troops. Hitler accepted this advice. Between 27 May and 4 June 338,000 British and French troops were got away by sea – the 'miracle of Dunkirk'. While this was going on, on 2 June, again at Charleville, Hitler addressed von Rundstedt and his generals and again praised Britain and her mission for the white race.

Hitler's Revenge and Triumph

ON 21 JUNE 1940, in a little clearing in the forest of Compiègne, Hitler, taking his revenge for the German capitulation in the same spot in 1918, humiliated the French politicians and generals. In the middle of the clearing was the original old railway Wagon-Lit of Marshal Foch, hauled out to its original location from the museum, whose walls the Germans had just pulled down. It was a lovely summer's day and the sun beat down on the elms, oaks, pines and cypresses surrounding the glade at Rethondes. At 3.15 p.m. Hitler and his entourage arrived in a caravan of black Mercedes. He wore a double-breasted grey military uniform; Göring wore his sky-blue Luftwaffe uniform; Generals Keitel and Brauchitsch wore field-grey uniforms; Grand Admiral Raeder wore a dark blue naval uniform. Rudolf Hess and Ribbentrop were there, but not Goebbels. They all read the inscription on the Alsace-Lorraine statue, which read (translated): 'Here on the eleventh of November 1918 succumbed the criminal pride of the German Empire – vanquished by the free peoples which it tried to enslave.' Hitler's face was seen to be 'afire with scorn, anger, hate, revenge, triumph.' Inside the railway carriage with the French delegation, led by General Charles Huntziger, Hitler pointedly sat in the seat Foch had occupied at the signing of the 1918 Armistice; then, as a snub to the French, he walked out, leaving Keitel to negotiate – or dictate – the terms of the new armistice.

Hitler's Art Tour

WITH A SMALL select group Hitler visited Paris – which had fallen on 14 June – early in the morning of 23 June 1940, accompanied by Speer, his invaluable architect; Lieutenant Wilhelm Brückner; Colonel (later General) Wilhelm Speidel (assigned by the new German Occupation Authority), and Arno Breker, Hitler's sculptor. The party flew to Le Bourget airfield and then went on Hitler's art tour in three large Mercedes cars. 'He seemed fascinated by the Opéra, went into ecstasies about its beauty, his eyes glittering, with an excitement that struck me as uncanny,' Speer wrote. Then they passed the Madeleine, the Arc de Triomphe and the Tomb of The Unknown Soldier, down the Champs-Élysées, the Trocadero, the Eiffel Tower, the Invalides (Hitler spent a long time examining Napoleon's tomb) and the Pantheon. Speer noted rather sadly that Hitler displayed little interest in the most beautiful works in Paris – Place des Vosges, the Louvre, Palais de Justice, Sainte-Chapelle. He did, however, became animated by the elegant houses in the Rue de Rivoli. By 9 a.m. the tour was over. Hitler told his group, 'It was the dream of my life to be permitted to see Paris. I cannot say how happy I am to have that dream fulfilled today.'

The Madagascar Plan

THE GERMAN FOREIGN OFFICE and the Central Office for Reich Security (*Reichssischerheitshauptamt*; or the RHSA) had developed a plan for deporting all European Jews to French-owned Madagascar. On 12 July 1940, after the fall of France, Hitler had given the go-ahead to plans for deportation and declared that France had to renounce the island. He wanted a 'forced ghetto' there, and accepted that there would be many casualties among the deportees. Hans Hinkel, head of the Jewish

✠ ⸻⸻⸻⸻⸻⸻⸻⸻⸻⸻⸻⸻⸻⸻⸻⸻ ✠

Section of the Propaganda Ministry, reported on 8 September that, provided transportation was available, the 72,000 Berlin Jews could be moved out in two months. On 17 September Hinkel reported to Hitler that to 'evacuate' 3.5 million European Jews to Madagascar required the successful ending of the war with Great Britain. Only in 1941 was the Madagascar plan abandoned.

The Thoughtful Duchess: Operation Willi

SINCE THE SELF-EXILED Duke of Windsor had met Hitler in 1937, he had been serving as a major-general with the British Military Mission near Paris. After the success in 1940 of Hitler's Operation Yellow in knocking France out of the war, the Windsors escaped France through Spain to Portugal. The Duke bitterly attacked Churchill's continuation of the war and foresaw that 'protracted heavy bombardment would make Britain ready for peace'. In July 1940 Ribbentrop set in motion the plan to kidnap the Duke – Operation Willi. He sent Walter Schellenberg (who became head of the SS Foreign Intelligence Department in 1941) to Lisbon to ensure that no harm came to the Duke, who was living in some style in a Portuguese banker's mansion. The Duke told Schellenberg of his loathing of Churchill and the war with Germany, and of his willingness to accept high office in a defeated Britain. The Windsors' passports had been impounded by the British Embassy in Lisbon, but Schellenberg arranged that they could cross into Spain if they wished. On 11 July Ribbentrop cabled the German Ambassador in Madrid that Germany would smooth the way for 'the Duke and Duchess to occupy the British throne'. The Duke replied that the British constitution forbade an abdicated monarch to return to the throne. The German emissary suggested that a conquered Britain would need a new constitution and 'the Duchess in particular became very thoughtful'. On 1 August the Windsors flew to the Bahamas.

A Revolution in Britain?

William Shirer, the American journalist for CBS, was allowed to visit all the Channel ports where the Wehrmacht were making preparations for Hitler's Directive No. 16, *Unternehmen Seelöwe* ('Operation Sealion'), for the invasion of England. On 21 July 1940 the Führer had told his generals in Berlin, 'England's situation is hopeless. The war has been won by us. A reversal of the prospects of success is impossible.' Shirer was amazed that all the preparations he saw along the coast were defensive, not offensive. When, on Hitler's orders, Göring launched *Unternehmen Adlerangriff* ('Operation Eagle Attack') he saw daily the Luftwaffe's aircraft leaving the French airfields for the huge onslaught against Britain of 15 and 16 August. But Berliners were stunned when, on the night of 25 August, the RAF bombed Berlin – which Göring had assured them was impossible. Hitler kept on deferring a decision to invade England and when on 16 September the RAF smashed a large German training exercise at sea, he did three things. He stepped up plans for Barbarossa, the invasion of Russia; he sanctioned indiscriminate mass bombing of London; and on 12 October he postponed *Seelöwe* until the spring of 1941. According to a senior officer in the OKW, Lieutenant-Colonel Bernhard von Lossberg, Hitler quite seriously expected a revolution to break out in Britain as a result of the devastating bombing of London.

Operation Moonlight Sonata

When the RAF bombed Munich, quite lightly, in early November 1940, Hitler personally demanded revenge for this insult. 'Operation Moonlight Sonata' was the codename for the Luftwaffe's attack by hundreds of bombers, which bombed Coventry on the night of 14 November. A 'pathfinder' squadron was equipped with an *X-Gerät*, or X-beam, radio-navigation system to guide them to their target. A continuous audible radio signal transmitted along the route to the target changed its note if the bomber strayed from its line; near the target a second and third beam cut across the first, indicating 'bombs away'. The problem was partly solved by a brilliant young scientific officer, R. V. Jones, who jammed or diverted the Luftwaffe's X-beam. Churchill called this 'the wizard war'.

Unlimited Power

GENERAL GOTTHARDT HEINRICI, a German officer but not a Nazi, noted a Hitler speech at the end of 1940 in which the Führer claimed that he was the first man since Charlemagne to hold unlimited power in his own hand. He did not, he said, hold the power in vain, but would know how to use it in a struggle for Germany. If war were not won, that would mean Germany had not stood the test of strength; in that case she would deserve to be, and would be, doomed.

Bunkers

WHEN THE RAF BOMBING RAIDS became heavier after the token efforts of 1940, Hitler issued orders for substantial bunkers to be built for his personal protection. As the reliability and weight of the British (and later American) bombs increased, so did the thickness of the concrete roofs of the bunkers. Eventually the concrete depth reached sixteen and a half feet. There were Hitler bunker systems built in Rastenburg, in Berlin, in Pullach near Munich, in the guest palace near Salzburg, at Obersalzberg, at the Bad Nauheim HQ, and, late in the war, in two underground HQs in the Silesian and Thuringian mountains. Biggest of all was the 'Giant' near Bad Charlottenbrunn, which cost 150 millions Reichmarks to build with its 328,000 cubic yards of reinforced concrete, 6 bridges, 36 miles of roads and 62 miles of pipes. Of course, all the Gauleiters – on orders from their Führer – had additional shelters and bunkers built for their safety. Göring built substantial underground installations at Carinhall and at Veldenstein near Nuremberg, and the 50-mile road from Carinhall to Berlin had to be provided with concrete shelters at regular intervals.

London's Burning

LATE IN 1940 Hitler made a speech in the Chancellery. 'Have you ever looked at a map of London? It is so closely built-up that one source of fire alone would suffice to destroy the whole city, as happened once before two hundred years ago. Göring wants to use innumerable incendiary bombs of an altogether new type to create sources of fire in all parts of London. Fires everywhere. Thousands of them. Then they'll unite in one gigantic area conflagration. Göring has the right idea. Explosive bombs don't work, but it can be done with incendiary bombs – total destruction of London.'

The Greatest Conqueror?

WILLIAM SHIRER watched in mounting horror and fascination as Hitler crushed the human spirit and freedom in Germany, persecuted the Jews and then destroyed them and anyone who opposed him, and dragged his nation towards war. Most Germans happily endorsed this 'Nazi barbarism'. Shirer observed the political, social and military scene, mainly in Berlin, from the summer of 1934 until December 1940, fifteen months after Hitler plunged Europe into war. 'When I departed Berlin, German troops, after their quick and easy conquests of Poland,

Denmark, Norway, Holland, Belgium and France, stood watch from the North Cape to the Pyrenees, from the Atlantic to beyond the Vistula. Britain stood alone. Few doubted that Hitler would emerge from the conflict as the greatest conqueror since Napoleon. Not many believed that Britain would survive.'

Hitler's Clockwork Precision

JOHN 'JOCK' COLVILLE, Churchill's Assistant Private Secretary, was a friend of Herschel Johnson, Minister at the American Embassy in London. Colville had an interesting thesis, that 'Hitler had been so impressed by the skill of his own staff work and by the speed and regularity with which his objects (up to July 1941) had been achieved, that he has ceased to believe anything impossible. Whereas our authorities are apt to take a gloomy view of an operation and in any case to prepare a very slow timetable, German [land] operations have invariably succeeded. German squadrons and divisions are moved from east to west or north to south in as many days as our forces require weeks. Thus I believe that Hitler did not contemplate the possibility of a check in Russia. Everything would work out with the same clockwork precision as before.'

The Unknown Painter

'I must say,' wrote Hitler in July 1941, 'I always enjoy meeting the Duce [Mussolini]. He's a great personality. It's curious to think that, at the same period as myself, he was working in the building trade in Germany . . . If the Duce were to die, it would be a great misfortune for Italy. As I walked with him in the gardens of the Villa Borghese, I could easily compare his profile with that of the Roman busts, and I realized he was one of the Caesars. There's no doubt at all that Mussolini is the heir of the great men of that period. Despite their weaknesses, the Italians have so many qualities that make us like them . . . The Italian people's musical sense . . . the beauty of its race! . . . The magic of Florence and Rome, of Ravenna, Siena, Perugia! Tuscany and Umbria, how lovely they are! . . . My dearest wish would be able to wander about in Italy as an unknown painter.'

One of the Jewels of Europe

FIELD MARSHAL GÜNTHER VON KLUGE asked Hitler on the evening of 29 October 1941 for his views on Paris, which he had visited the year before.

'I was very happy,' the Führer said, 'to think that there was at least one city in the Reich that was superior to Paris from the point of view of taste – I mean, Vienna. The old part of Paris gives a feeling of complete distinction. The great vistas are imposing . . . At present Berlin doesn't exist, but one day she'll be more beautiful than Paris . . . It was a relief to me that we weren't obliged to destroy Paris . . . Every finished work is of value as an example . . . The Ring in Vienna would not exist without the Paris boulevards. It's a copy of them.'

Hitler approved of the Invalides, the Madeleine, the Paris Opéra, the Eiffel Tower, but found Sacré-Coeur appalling and the Panthéon a horrible disappointment (the busts were all right, but the sculptures!). 'But, on the whole, Paris remains one of the jewels of Europe.'

'That Cunning Caucasian'

THREE WEEKS AFTER the successful launch of Operation Barbarossa on 22 June 1941, Hitler told his dinner companions, 'Stalin is one of the most extraordinary figures in world history. He began as a small clerk, and he has never stopped being a clerk. Stalin owes nothing to rhetoric [unlike the speaker]. He governs from his office, thanks to a bureaucracy that obeys his every nod and gesture. It's striking that Russian propaganda, in the criticisms it makes of us, always holds itself within certain limits. Stalin, that cunning Caucasian, is apparently quite ready to abandon European Russia, if he thinks that a failure to solve her problems would cause him to lose everything. Let nobody think Stalin might reconquer Europe from the Urals . . . This is the catastrophe that will cause the loss of the Soviet Empire.'

Hitler's armies had made extraordinary progress in Barbarossa and it looked as though Moscow would be taken by Christmas 1941. But when Stalin's son was captured Hitler ordered that he should be given especially good treatment.

Hitler on Jewry

AT DINNER on 25 October 1941 Hitler told his guests, Heinrich Himmler and Reinhard Heydrich: 'From the rostrum of the Reichstag I prophesied to Jewry that in the event of war's proving inevitable, the Jew would disappear from Europe. That race of criminals has on its conscience the two million dead of the first World War and now already hundreds of thousands more. Let nobody tell me that all the same we can't park them in the marshy parts of Russia! Who's worrying about our troops? It's not a bad idea, by the way, that public rumour attributes to us a plan to exterminate the Jews. Terror is a salutary thing. The attempt to create a Jewish State will be a failure.'

By 1941 there were already many concentration camps, including Ravensbrück and Auschwitz. Himmler himself ordered that Birkenau in Poland should become a killing centre for Russian officers, and that Chelmno, also in Poland, should be the first extermination camp: both of these earlier in 1941, before the cosy little supper party with the Führer.

'THE FASTER WE GO THE FASTER AWAY IT GETS'

Hess's Dramatic Exit

ON THE NIGHT of 10 May 1941, a Scots farmer was more than a little surprised to come across a German in Luftwaffe uniform and with a broken ankle. The man said to him in careful English, 'I have an important message for the Duke of Hamilton.' He was quickly arrested. Earlier that evening Rudolf Hess – anxious, it is thought, to impress his Führer by sealing a peace agreement with Britain – and thus ensuring a German victory – had suddenly and secretly flown to Scotland and parachuted in to talk peace terms with the Duke of Hamilton.

Hitler, Göring, Ribbentrop and Bormann were horrified when they learned of his action, and more than a little worried. 'If Hess really gets there just imagine: Churchill has Hess in his grasp! What lunacy on Hess's part. They will give Hess some drug or other to make him stand before a microphone and broadcast whatever Churchill wants,' was Hitler's immediate panicky reaction. After ten attempts at an official communiqué Hitler insisted on the inclusion of the phrase 'it was the action of a madman'. The British had in any case quickly come to the same conclusion – even if he was not mad, he was certainly mentally ill. Hess had been at Hitler's side since the Great War: served in the same regiment, marched with him in the Beer Hall putsch, was in prison with him at Landsberg, he was a very close friend and colleague. The whole world was astonished. In the event, Hess achieved nothing and remained in captivity for the rest of his life, dying in Spandau prison, Berlin, in 1987. Hitler later always emphasized how much 'he had esteemed his friend, upright and honest until he was led astray.'

The Path to War with America

PRESIDENT ROOSEVELT'S naval policy was to keep the sea routes open to Europe and not to be intimidated by Hitler's submarine blockade. The March 1941 Lend-Lease Agreement, largely negotiated between Roosevelt and Churchill, meant a stream of American and British merchant ships carrying cargo across the North Atlantic, which in turn spurred on Hitler's U-boat fleet. Admiral Raeder wanted to attack US merchant shipping, which Hitler flatly refused to consider. In September 1941 the US destroyer *Greer* was attacked by a U-boat, and in retaliation laid a total of nineteen depth charges, making her the first US ship to fire on a German vessel in that war. Although the US was not to enter the war officially for another three months, this incident prompted Roosevelt to give the US navy a 'shoot on sight' order. In October the USS *Kearney* was attacked and the USS *Reuben James* sunk. On 28 November the Japanese were suggesting a military alliance with Germany for a war against the USA and Great Britain. On 4 December Hitler had already decided to go to war against America, hoping that the Americans would have to fight two naval wars – against Germany and Japan – giving him more time to finalize the Russian campaign. Nevertheless, the news on 7 December of the Japanese attack on the American Pacific fleet at Pearl Harbor came as a complete surprise to Hitler (as it did to Churchill). On 11 December Ribbentrop was ordered to tell the American chargé d'affaires, Leland B. Morris, that Germany was now at war with the USA. Hitler then told the Reichstag that war had been declared, blaming Roosevelt for provoking the conflict. Goebbels was delighted and said, 'The USA will need all their military weapons to fight Japan, not supply England.' Hitler then signed the German-Italian-Japanese tripartite agreement with the 'unshakeable decision' not to lay down their arms until the war against the USA and Britain was won.

A Führer Rage

GENERAL HEINZ GUDERIAN (1885–1954) was Hitler's leading armoured-warfare expert. While Field Marshall Erwin Rommel will be remembered for his Afrikakorps successes, and ultimate failure, in North Africa, and perhaps for his short lived command in Normandy, but Guderian's record in command of armour in Poland, the Low Countries, France and Russia was far superior. Blunt and outspoken to Hitler's face in his criticisms of the other's decisions, he describes a Führer rage. 'His fists raised, his cheeks flushed with anger, his whole body trembling, the man stood in front of me beside himself with fury, having lost all self-control. After each outburst Hitler would stride up and down the carpet edge, then suddenly stop immediately in front of me and hurl his next accusation in my face. He was almost screaming, his eyes seemed almost to pop out of his head and the veins stood out on his temples.' On Christmas Day 1941 Hitler fired Guderian for carrying out a sensible withdrawal in contravention of Hitler's specific order. He was reinstated in March 1943, became Army Chief of Staff and was fired again by Hitler on 28 March 1945. It took immense personal bravery to stand up to the Führer, and many who did so ended up in concentration camps – or worse.

Syphilis

THERE IS an unpleasant chapter in *Mein Kampf* about syphilis, and it is possible that Hitler associated with prostitutes during his time in Vienna. He certainly insisted on taking Gustl Kubizek on a tour of the red-light district.

Hitler's medical condition has been debated extensively; it is thought that he contracted syphilis in Vienna before the First World War and by the 1940s was suffering badly from its effect. His mania in his last years is considered indicative of the condition and he had an abnormal heartbeat that suggests syphilitic aortitis. The diary kept by Dr Theodor Morell, his favourite doctor, gives some circumstantial evidence. Hitler was prone to encephalitis, dizziness, flatulence, neck pustules, chest pain, gastric pain and restrictive palsies, which are all symptoms of syphilis.

Morell was dismissed by Hitler in 1944 when his medical rivals gained the upper hand. He buried his diaries near his private bunker at Bad Reichenhall at the end of the war. Captured by the Allies, but not prosecuted, he died in 1948.

Hitler's Peace Feelers

IN 1941 the British government issued a report to Britain's Ambassador to the United States, Lord Halifax, for confidential transmission to President Roosevelt, on no fewer than sixteen peace attempts made by the German government between the summers of 1939 and 1941. Some came with Hitler's overt blessing, some more deviously through intermediaries in Sweden, Switzerland, Spain or Portugal. Amongst the intermediaries were the Papal Nuncio, King Gustav V of Sweden, the German Ambassador in Washington and General Franco. Lord Halifax had been privy to many of these peace feelers in his previous capacity as Foreign Secretary. Hitler's 'players' included Hitler's personal legal advisor Dr Ludwig Weissauer, Josef Goebbels, Reichsbank president Hjalmar Schacht, former German War Minister Dr Gessler, Herman Göring and Heinrich Himmler (four times). But from the moment that Winston Churchill became Prime Minister in May 1940, the answer was categorically negative.

The Führer's Peasant Shadow – 'Mephistopheles'

A GREY, inconspicuous, hardworking, crafty bureaucrat, Reichsleiter Martin Bormann was Hitler's shadow from 1934 onwards.

Initially secretary to Hess, he wormed his way into becoming indispensable to Hitler, and by 1942 he had, with Hitler's compliance, succeeded in winning control of his Führer's appointments calendar. No civilian members of the government or Party, including ministers, Reichsleiters and Gauleiters, could gain access to Hitler without Bormann's approval. Bormann also controlled Hitler's personal finances, so that even Eva Braun had to ask him for maintenance funds. The vast building complex of Hitler's Obersalzberg was under his control. The military chieftains could gain access easily through Hitler's three or four military adjutants, although their purse-strings were controlled by Bormann. He accompanied his master on every trip and never left his side in the Chancellery until Hitler went to bed early in the morning. On 12 April 1943 Bormann became officially 'Secretary to the Führer'. He was hardworking, reliable and ultimately indispensable. However, Speer thought that he was a brutal, coarse, uncultured subordinate who behaved like a peasant. His nickname was 'Mephistopheles'.

On Women

'At this period [1925] I knew a lot of women. Several of them became attached to me. Why then didn't I marry? To leave a wife behind me? At the slightest imprudence, I ran the risk of going back to prison for six years. So there could be no question of marriage for me. I therefore had to renounce certain opportunities that offered themselves.'

And again later, in 1942, looking back Hitler remarked, 'It's lucky I'm not married. For me, marriage would have been a disaster. There's a point at which misunderstanding is bound to arise between man and wife; it's when the husband cannot give his wife all the time she feels entitled to demand. As long as only other couples are involved, one hears women say: "I don't understand Frau So-and-so. *I* wouldn't behave like that." But when she herself is involved, every woman is unreasonable to the same degree. One must understand this demandingness. A woman who loves her husband lives only for his sake. That's why, in her turn, she expects her spouse to live likewise for *her* sake. It's only after maternity that the woman discovers that other realities exist in life for her. The man, on the other hand, is a slave to his thoughts. The idea of his duties rules him. He necessarily has moments when he wants to throw the whole thing overboard, wife and children too.'

Henchmen in Disarray

TOWARDS THE END OF 1942 Hitler's coterie of powerful ministers split into two groups in competition with each other. Martin Bormann was allied with Field Marshal Keitel and Hans Lammers (Reich Minister and chief of the Reich Chancellery) to form the 'Council of Three'. Goebbels, Speer, Walter Funk, Minister for Economic Affairs, and Robert Ley, who all had academic university backgrounds formed, with Göring's support, a loose bloc with the object of curbing the Council of Three's increasing control of access to the Führer. Hitler's almost total preoccupation with the running of the war front meant that the political, economic and social control of the German people was being usurped by the Council of Three. Himmler, the most dangerous man in Germany, controlled the brutal SS activities in Germany and the occupied territories and was almost a law unto himself. Göring, still Hitler's No. 2 and successor-designate, was now losing his control over his morphine addiction (which had originated in the injury he received during the Munich putsch) and had become enormously fat (a side effect of the morphine addiction); preferring to devote himself to his magnificent collection of looted jewellery and paintings, he was a shadow of his earlier brilliant self. As the Luftwaffe failed increasingly to protect German cities from the RAF Göring was frequently in disgrace with Hitler.

Stalin: 'Half Beast, Half Giant'

THE FAILURE to capture Moscow had changed Hitler's attitude to Stalin. In July 1942 Hitler told his dinner guests, 'The arms and equipment of the Russian armies are the best proof of its efficiency in the handling of industrial manpower. Stalin, too, must command our unconditional respect. In his own way he is a hell of a fellow! He knows his models, Genghis Khan and the others, very well, and the scope of his industrial planning is exceeded only by our own Four-Year Plan.' Hitler was sure that Stalin would create total employment unlike such 'capitalist States as the United States of America'. A month later, on 9 August 1942, he was telling three Gauleiters over the evening meal that 'had it not been for the mud and rain last October, we should have been in Moscow in no time. We have now learnt that the moment the rain comes, we must stop everything . . . Stalin is half beast, half giant. To the social side of life he is utterly indifferent. The people can rot, for all he cares. If we had given him another ten years, Europe would have been swept away . . . Without the German Wehrmacht, it would have been all up with Europe even now.'

Hitler: 'Extraordinarily Humane' to Jews

THE SPECIAL GUESTS for lunch with their Führer on 23 January 1942 were Himmler, Hans Heinrich Lammers (1879–1962), Head of Administration in the Reich Chancellery, and Colonel Kurt Zeitzler, Chief of the Army General Staff. Hitler told them, 'The Jew must clear out of Europe. Otherwise no understanding will be possible between Europeans. It's the Jew who prevents everything. When I think about it, I realize that I'm extraordinarily humane . . . For my part, I restrict myself to telling them they must go away . . . But if they refuse to go voluntarily, I see no other solution but extermination . . . Why did the Jew provoke this war?'

The Wannsee Conference (see below) – to discuss 'the Jew' – had been held three days before, on 20 January.

Hitler's Military Situation Conference

FROM THE OUTBREAK OF WAR in 1939 Hitler dominated all the main static campaigns, particularly on the Russian front. There was a distinct pattern to his situation conferences. They started every day at noon and lasted two or three hours. Hitler was the only person seated, usually in an armchair with a rush seat, and the chosen participants stood around the large map table. The key figures, Keitel, Modl and Zeitzler, often Himmler, sometimes Göring (who had an upholstered stool on which to place his corpulent frame), all the adjutants, Army General Staff and Waffen SS staff and liaison officers attended. Desk lamps on long articulated arms illuminated the maps. First the eastern theatre of war would be discussed. Three or four strategic maps pasted together, each of them about eight feet by five feet, were laid out in front of Hitler. Every detail of the previous day was entered on the maps, every advance, even minor patrols, and the Chief of Staff explained each entry. Bit by bit the maps were pushed further up the table – longer discussions were devoted to the important situations. The 'Bohemian corporal', as Hitler was sometimes derogatively known, pushed divisions back and forth. He revelled in petty details. He thought that by scrutiny of maps and the terrain they showed he could influence the battlefronts. And of course strategic withdrawals were never allowed. Very few of his generals dared stand up to him.

Hitler's Party Treasurer and Book Keeper

FRANZ XAVER SCHWARZ (1875–1947) joined the Nazi Party in 1922; a bookkeeper by training, he was well suited to helping restore the Party's fortunes following the failed Munich putsch. One of the first few members of the new and much-reduced NSDAP, he became Party Treasurer in March 1925 and remained so until the Party's demise in 1945. This short, plump, bald, pedantic man controlled membership subscriptions and built up the Party's funds. He came to be one of Hitler's 'old comrades' and a member of the close circle. In April 1929, when Hitler (it has been claimed) wrote a very explicit letter to his niece Geli Raubal, which fell into a blackmailer's hands, Schwarz arranged the required pay-off. In the 1934 'thank-you notes' Schwarz came second, behind Hess, in Hitler's list of thirteen main supporters, although Martin Bormann had started to take control of Hitler's personal finances. On a February evening in 1942 Hitler told Himmler,'It's unbelievable what the Party owes Schwarz. It was thanks to the good order in which he kept our finances that we were able to develop so rapidly and wipe out the other parties. Schwarz only reports to me once a year.' Hitler was delighted that he need not bother about affairs of administration. Three years later Schwarz burned all Party financial documents in the Brown House, the NSDAP's headquarters in Munich.

The Wannsee Conference

IN THE SS RSHA headquarters at a villa in Wannsee, Berlin, one of the most notorious meetings of the twentieth century took place. On 20 January 1942 a number of Hitler's lesser henchmen – high-ranking government and Nazi Party officials but not Hitler's immediate circle — gathered together to plan the 'Final Solution', the extermination of the Jewish population of the Third Reich and of Europe. It was carefully managed. Hitler passed the buck to his No.2, Hermann Göring, who passed the buck to Himmler, head of the SS, who in turn ducked out and made Reinhard Heydrich, head of the RSHA, chairman of the meeting. The others there were: Josef Bühler, the State Secretary; Adolf Eichmann, the RSHA deportation expert, who took the minutes; Dr Roland Freisler, Minister of Justice; Otto Hoffman for the Race and Resettlement Main Office; Dr Gerhard Klopfer (NSDAP Chancellery); Friedrich Wilhelm Kritzinger (Reich Chancellery); SS-Sturmbannführer Dr Rudolf Lange, SD (Intelligence) Commander for Latvia; Dr George Leibbrandt (Reich Ministry for the Occupied Eastern Territories); Martin Franz Julius Luther (Foreign Office); Gauleiter Dr Alfred Meyer (Reich Ministry for the Occupied Eastern territories); the Gestapo chief, Heinrich Müller; Erich Neumann, Director, Office of the Four-Year Plan; Karl Schöngarth (SD); and Dr Wilhelm Stückart, Minister of the Interior – fifteen in all. Himmler's plan was to spread the responsibility across as many departments as possible. At no point was killing mentioned – the word used was 'resettled'; Jews were to be 'resettled', and directives were agreed to move them all to the east as part of the 'territorial solution'. Heydrich's view was that the vast labour pool in the east created by these deportations would be used for road building and construction projects (albeit with a high death rate).

The Wannsee Conference was a key stepping stone to the 'Final Solution'. All fifteen representatives of the Third Reich were thus guilty of orchestrating mass murder.

Nuclear Research, Stage 2

GOEBBELS'S DIARY of 21 March 1942 noted, 'Research into the realm of atomic destruction has now proceeded to a point where results may possibly be used in the present war. It is essential that we should keep ahead of everybody.'

General Friedrich Fromm, Chief of Army Armaments, suggested to Albert Speer in April 1942 that the only chance of Germany winning the war lay in developing a weapon with totally new effects. From 1937 to 1940 the army had spent 550 million Reichmarks on the development of a large rocket which produced, at Peenemünde, the first V (for Vengeance) weapons. On 6 May 1942 Speer proposed to Hitler that Göring be placed at the head of the Reich Research Council, thus emphasizing its importance. Speer chaired a meeting at Harnack House, the Berlin centre of the Kaiser Wilhelm Gesellschaft (the Kaiser Wilhelm Society for the Advancement of Science), with Field Marshal Erhard Milch, armaments chief of the Luftwaffe, General Fromm, Admiral Karl Witzell and various scientists, including Nobel Prize-winners Otto Hahn and Werner Heisenberg. Professor Heisenberg was bitter about the lack of support for nuclear research in Germany.

Hitler Denies his Roots

DRIVING FROM BUDWEIS to Krems in 1942 Speer noticed a large plaque on a house in the village of Spital, close to the Czech border. The wording on it read 'The Führer lived here in his youth.' Speer later mentioned this to Hitler, who flew into a rage and shouted for Martin Bormann, who hurried in, scared. Hitler snarled at him, Bormann reported, 'How many times had he said that this village [Spital] must never be mentioned. That idiot of a Gauleiter had gone and put up a plaque. It must be removed at once.' Hitler was ashamed of his father and of his early upbringing. Linz and Braunau 'roots' were fine, but not Spital where Alois Schicklgruber, born illegitimately, had lived.

A few years later, Hitler's legal advisor and a Nazi Party member, Hans Frank, passed the time before his execution for crimes against humanity by writing an account of his life. In it he alleged that in 1930 Hitler had commissioned him to investigate his unknown grandfather. Frank claimed to have discovered that the grandfather was a young Austrian Jew named Frankenberger for whose family Hitler's grandmother, Maria Anna Schicklgruber, worked as a housemaid. She had given birth on 7 June 1837 in House 13, Strones, in the Austrian Walviertel region, to Alois, who would become Hitler's father. Maria subsequently married Johann Georg Hiedler, but it was not until 1876 that Alois Schicklgruber, aged nearly forty, took his birth certificate to the local priest, who agreed to make an illegal entry in the blank space, spelling the required name of Hiedler as Hitler. He was now officially Alois Hitler. There is, however, no concrete evidence of Frank having passed his 'discoveries' on to Hitler, or of any connection with a family called Frankenberger.

Johann Georg himself could have been the father – or perhaps his married brother, Johann Nepomuk Hiedler, with whom Alois went to live . . . in Spital. Adolf's mother – Alois's third wife – was Johann Nepomuk's granddaughter.

It seems certain that Hitler was worried that something damaging might be found out about his ancestry – at worst that his grandfather had been Jewish; or that he was born of an incestuous relationship, which, combined with accounts of insanity in the family, had serious implications. Altogether an embarrassment for the leader of a party whose aim was to 'maintain the purity of the German Master Race'.

Churchill Stirring up Trouble

DESPITE Hess's unilateral action to seek a peaceful solution via the Duke of Hamilton, Hitler still did not know the true state of

British politicians' resolve to keep on fighting. But thanks to the work of the propaganda wing (SO1) of Britain's Special Operations Executive (SOE), and its use of many intermediaries, Hitler had been encouraged to believe that Lord Halifax might move to oust Churchill from the premiership and negotiate an armistice with Germany. SO1, renamed the Political Warfare Executive or PWE, was now under the leadership of Churchill's staunch friend, Brendan Bracken. One of its activities was to try to lure Himmler, via his trusted Schellenberg, to sue for peace and perhaps overthrow Hitler in the process. Himmler made half a dozen efforts via Stockholm and Madrid to establish a 'concordat'; Churchill had, of course, no intention of signing a peace agreement. But the PWE continued its efforts to stir up trouble among the Führer's top brass.

Nuclear Research, Stage 3

THE NOBEL PRIZE-WINNING PHYSICIST Professor Werner Heisenberg reported in 1942 on 'atom smashing' and the development of the uranium machine and the cyclotron – a particle accelerator or atom-smashing machine. He declared that Germany had found the scientific solution to nuclear fission and that, theoretically, building an atomic bomb was possible, *but* there was a lack of funds and materials, and scientific men should be drafted into the nuclear research services. There was only one cyclotron in Europe – it was in Paris and had minimal capacity. Speer said that ample funds were available and General Fromm offered to release several hundred scientists from the services. However, it was clear to Speer that they could not count on anything for three or four years, and the war would certainly have been decided long before then.

Hitler's Bedtime Story

THE EBULLIENT piano-playing Putzi Hanfstängl eventually annoyed Hitler so much that, after a curious episode in which Putzi was apparently sent to Spain on a special mission, requiring him to parachute into a danger zone, and was – possibly – saved by the pilot making a fake emergency landing, he was exiled by Hitler. He managed to reach London where he was interned before being sent to Canada. In 1942 the Canadians turned him over to the US, where, as a valuable prisoner – the half-American friend of Hitler – he was asked (or rather, ordered) to write a report, which ran to 68 pages, covering every aspect of the Führer's life and character. A US government psychologist provided a checklist, which *inter alia*, included religion, women, art, music, literature, sexuality and friendships. The American G-2 military intelligence staff gave Hanfstängl's opus the codename 'S-Project', the 'S' standing for Sedgwick, one of Putzi's influential family connections. They wanted to know Hitler's strengths: gift of oratory, leadership, military skills; and his weaknesses: 'divide and conquer', childhood poverty, anti-Semitic and anti-Communist phobias, occult sympathies. When the report was shown to President Roosevelt on 3 December 1942 he christened it 'Hitler's bedtime story'.

Hitler's Charisma

TRAUDL JUNGE, aged twenty-two in 1942, was the youngest and last of Hitler's secretaries. She wrote in her book *Until the Final Hour*, 'It is hard to recreate or imagine the mesmeric effect Hitler had on everyone he encountered. Even people bitterly opposed to him commented on the power he radiated, how they felt irresistibly drawn to him even though it made them feel troubled and guilty afterwards. This phenomenon is often present in extremely powerful men when they choose to exert their charm – and charm – or even more dangerously, charisma, rather than the emanation of evil, was Hitler's most obvious characteristic.' Traudl Junge felt that when Hitler went away from her and her colleagues 'some essential element was missing, even oxygen, an awareness of being alive – there was a – vacuum.'

Stalingrad – 'The Old Mistakes Again'

THE SOVIET ARMIES encircling Stalingrad smashed through the Romanian divisions and Hitler made slighting remarks about the fighting qualities of his allies. Shortly afterwards, on 19 November 1942, the Soviets began overwhelming German divisions as well. Another Soviet offensive, in a pincer movement, trapped the German armies around Stalingrad. Göring promised solemnly to supply the German troops in the pocket by air. Hitler's generals, Zeitzler and Keitel, tried to persuade him that the Sixth Army under Field Marshall Friedrich Paulus should fight their way out to freedom, i.e. retreat, but Hitler, who was in the Berghof, simply did not understand the gravity of the situation and said, 'Our generals are making their old mistakes again. They always over-estimate the strength of the Russians. According to all the frontline reports the enemy's human material is no longer sufficient. They are weakened. They have lost far too much blood. But of course nobody wants to accept such reports. Besides, how badly Russian officers are trained. No offensive can be organized with such officers. We know what it takes! In the short or long run the Russians will simply come to a halt. They'll run down. Meanwhile we shall throw in a few fresh divisions – that will put things right.' Hitler had been right over the 1940 blitzkrieg in the Low Countries and France and his doubting generals had been proved wrong. This time they were right and he was wrong. On 30 January 1943 Paulus, with twenty-four generals and 90,000 surviving German soldiers, surrendered. It was a catastrophe for the Third Reich.

Hitler's Table Talk

ON 7 JULY 1941 a Party official, Heinrich Heim, was asked by Hitler to sit discreetly in a corner and take brief shorthand notes of the Führer's monologues. The typed record was then handed to Martin Bormann, who read through the day's offering, making comments, clarifying various points, and then initialled and filed it. From 11 March 1942 Heim was temporarily replaced for a four-month period by Dr Henry Picker. Altogether 328 'sessions' were recorded, the last being on 29–30 November 1944. Eventually 1,045 typed pages were completed and kept in Bormann's personal custody. Of the two eventual copies made, one was passed to Party archives in Munich, which were later destroyed by fire, and the other survived with Frau Bormann, and was known as 'Bormann – *Vermeke* [Notes]'. Eventually this was passed to François Genoud, a Swiss financier and Nazi backer. Despite a court case against Henry Picker, who authorized a French edition, Genoud sold the British book rights to Weidenfeld & Nicolson. Edited by Hugh Trevor-Roper, it was duly published as a book in 1953 under the title *Hitler's Table Talk*.

Hitler's Carte Blanche

ADDRESSING THE REICHSTAG on 26 April 1942, Hitler asked for total *carte blanche*. 'I do, however, expect one thing: that the nation give me the right to take immediate action in any way I see fit, wherever I do not find the obedience unconditionally called for by service of the greater cause. This is a matter of life and

Stalin and Roosevelt give the Führer a thrashing in Russia and Africa.

death to us [wild applause]. At the front and at home, in transport, civil service and the judiciary there must be obedience to only one idea, namely the fight for victory [wild applause].' It was the last time the Reichstag would ever meet. Hitler was the law.

Hitler's Favourite Painters

SOME OF HITLER'S favourite painters were:

Franz Stuck (1863–1928) who painted erotic oils with big-busted women, grotesque devils, snakes, dwarfs, under titles such as *Salome*, *Siren with a Harp*, and many others;

Eduard Grützner (1846–1925), whose pictures of tipsy monks and butlers fascinated Hitler. 'Look at these details, Grützner is greatly underrated. It's simply that he hasn't been discovered yet [1933]. Some day he'll be worth as much as a Rembrandt.' Hitler claimed to have the largest collection of Grützner in Germany;

Carl Spitzweg (1808–85) was another favourite, a painter who mocked the small-town Munich of his period. *The Poet*, *Nepal* and *Serenade* were amongst thirty Spitzwegs owned by Hitler.

Adolf Ziegler (1829–1959), Friedrich Stahl, Hans Thoma (1839–1924) and Wilhelm Leibl (1844–1900) were long-forgotten painters rediscovered and acquired in considerable numbers by the Führer. From the dealer Karl Haberstock he purchased a Rubens, a Watteau, a Canaletto, a Bordone, a van Dyck and a Boecklin.

Hitler's Information Network

BRITAIN HAS ALWAYS taken great pride in the success of the Bletchley Park ULTRA team who 'read' with conspicuous success the German Enigma radio codes. Hitler's intake of information was equally staggering. During 1941 Ambassador Walther Hewel logged 1,100 different diplomatic papers passed to his Führer for information and action. In the first quarter of 1942 there were 800 more. FA (*Forschungsamt* – Himmler's 'Research Office') wiretaps were the main source, but the German Post Office was now unscrambling the radio-telephone link between London and Washington. Transcripts included top-secret talks between Churchill and Roosevelt. Stalin's despatches from Moscow to Yugoslavia and Turkey were read. American telegrams from Cairo to Washington provided Rommel with key Allied plans including those for a projected invasion of north-west Africa. Allied diplomatic messages out of Madrid and Lisbon were routinely fed back to Hitler, including Mountbatten's plan for an amphibious attack on the French mainland at Dieppe. British historians have underestimated Hitler's sources of information after the German spies in the UK were rounded up in 1938–40.

Goebbels Sang for his Supper

JOSEPH GOEBBELS (1897–1945) became an ardent admirer of Hitler during the 1923 Munich putsch trial. Goebbels was short, unattractive and embittered by his disabilities: his crippled left leg made him unfit for war service. He was a university graduate, which was unusual in the Hitler circles, and wrote for the *Völkischer Beobachter*. He became Gauleiter of Berlin and in 1928, Nazi Party propaganda chief, and introduced the greeting 'Heil Hitler!' to the Party and to the nation (he always grovelled shamelessly to his Führer). Thus he made himself indispensable to Hitler. The Nuremberg rallies and all other major Nazi military rallies were stage-managed by Goebbels. Soon he controlled all film, radio, theatre, music, painting, dance and sculpture in the Third Reich, and in March 1935 he introduced the world's first regular TV service, as well as sponsoring a cheap 'people's' radio set. It was he who issued orders for the

Kristalnacht anti-Semitic riots. He also engaged the renegade William Joyce, 'Lord Haw-Haw', to make anti-British radio broadcasts. Goebbels enjoyed a luxurious lifestyle but also supported his wife, many children and various mistresses.

One evening in mid-March 1943 he and Speer supped with Hitler, who had had a fire lit in the fireplace. An orderly brought in a bottle of wine, and Fachinger mineral water for Hitler. Speer observed how Goebbels knew how to entertain. He spoke in brilliant polished phrases, with irony in the right place and admiration where Hitler expected it, with sentimentality when the moment and subject required it, with gossip and the love affairs of his actress friends. He mixed everything in a masterly brew – movies, theatre, old times, details of the Goebbels family and children. Stories of their games and innocent remarks distracted Hitler from his cares of state; his self assurance was strengthened and his vanity flattered. Perhaps surprisingly, Hitler reciprocated by magnifying his Propaganda Minister's achievements; Goebbels certainly sang for his supper. Speer noted, a trifle sourly, 'The leaders of the Third Reich were fond of mutual praise.'

Hitler and the Secret Weapons (1)

THE PEENEMÜNDE SCIENTISTS, under Wernher von Braun's genius, had developed a guided flying bomb; a rocket-powered aircraft much faster than a jet; a rocket missile that homed in on an enemy aircraft by tracking the heat rays from its engines; a torpedo that reacted to sound and could pursue a fleeing ship; and a ground-to-air missile to destroy Allied bombers. But Hitler was in a dilemma. He had to make a crucial decision as there was only the industrial capacity to make one of these. Should it be the A-4 (the V-2), a 46-foot-long rocket weighing 13 metric tonnes which could rain terror on England? Or should they develop the Waterfall, a 25-foot-long, radio-controlled anti-aircraft missile with a 500-pound warhead, which could reach 50,000 feet and had, in daylight, a near certainty of destroying an Allied bomber? Hitler wavered: 2,210 scientists and engineers worked at Peenemünde on the V-2s and only 220 on Waterfall. London and the south-east of England survived the V-2s, and the Allied bombers over Germany survived the very few Waterfalls.

The Hitler Diet

DR KARL BRANDT was the Führer's favourite doctor. Others included Professors Werner Haase and Hanskarl von Hasselbach. Dr Theodor Morell was always on hand to give him shots of dextrose, hormones or vitamins. Stomach cramps induced by nerves were the most frequent ailment. In May 1943 Brandt, on the advice of Marshal Antonescu, the national leader of Romania, recommended a Viennese dietician, Frau Marlene von Exner, who was attractive, young and good-natured. Hitler adored her, and with her recalled happy memories of life in Vienna. For Antonescu she produced caviar, oysters, mayonnaise and other delicacies, but Hitler's strict diet was a problem. A typical menu prepared for him by her was orange juice with linseed gruel, rice pudding with herb sauce and crispbread with nut and butter paste.

The Wolfsschanze

HITLER spent more than 800 days and nights in his 'Wolf's Lair' HQ on the East Prussian border during the Second World War. The huge HQ bunker complex at Rastenberg was a purely military base. Nearly fifty staff including Hitler's four female secretaries lived like rats – the food was indifferent, the air stale and fetid, there was high humidity in the summer and it was beastly cold in the winter. The thick pine forests were sinister and claustrophobic and the tormenting mosquitoes were so pervasive that Hitler had to wear a special protective helmet, like a beekeeper's, for protection.

The Spent Old Man

NEARLY FIFTY-FOUR and under immense pressure after defeats in North Africa and Russia, in March 1943 Hitler appeared to be 'a spent old man . . . He stared fixedly into space through bulging eyes, his cheeks were blotchy and his spine was twisted by kyphosis and a light scoliosis. His left arm and leg twitched and he dragged his feet. He became increasingly excitable, reacted violently to criticism and stuck obstinately to his own opinions, however ludicrous. He spoke in a dull monotone, repeated himself and liked to harp on his childhood and early career.' His doctors persuaded him to try to take three months' rest, and he did in fact spend two five-week periods away from the Wolfsschanze and Werwolf (Russian HQ near Vinnitsa in the Ukraine), back at the Berghof retreat.

'Whoever Rules Europe . . .'

JUST AFTER Paulus surrendered a German army at Stalingrad and while a similar disaster was happening in North Africa, Goebbels noted in his diary on 8 May 1943, 'The Führer expresses his unshakeable conviction that the Reich will one day rule all of Europe. We will have to survive a great many conflicts but they will doubtless lead to the most glorious triumphs. And from then on the road to world domination is practically spread out before us. For whoever rules Europe will be able to seize the leadership of the world.' On 24 June Hitler told his supper companions, 'I feel equally at home anywhere in the Reich, and my love for all Germans [85 million of them] is equal, as long as they do not range themselves against the interests of the Reich, of which I am the guardian. In this respect I behave as if I am in the midst of my family.'

'Very Pale and Exceptionally Jumpy'

THEODOR MORELL (1890–1948), who was Hitler's doctor for nine years until 1944, originally diagnosed the hypochondriac Führer as suffering from 'intestinal exhaustion', which appealed to the health crank in Hitler. Morell specialized in all kinds of strange treatments such as bull's testicles, but also, and, more dangerously, he favoured giving amphetamines and opium-based painkillers. Morell's treatments may have contributed to Hitler's later condition that resembled Parkinson's disease. On Sunday 18 July 1943 Hitler planned to meet Mussolini. According to Morell, 'Führer had me sent for at ten-thirty a.m., said he has had the most violent stomach pains since three a.m. and hasn't slept a wink. His abdomen is as taut as a board, full of gas, with no palpation pains anywhere. Looking *very* pale and exceptionally jumpy: facing a vital conference with the Duce in Italy tomorrow. Diagnosis: *spastic constipation* caused by overwork over the last few days – three days with virtually no sleep, one conference after another and working far into the night. – Last night he ate white cheese and roll-ups (*Rolladen*) with spinach and peas.

'As he can't duck out of some important conferences and decisions before his departure at three-thirty p.m., no narcotics can be given him; I can only give him an intravenous injection of one ampoule of Eupaverin [a muscle relaxant], some gentle stomach massage, two Euflat pills [for heartburn/stomach or intestinal complaints] and three spoons of olive oil. Last night he took five Leo pills [a laxative].Before leaving for the airfield I gave him an intramuscular injection of an ampoule of Eukodal [morphine-based painkiller]. He was looking very bad and rather faint.'

The Secret German-Russian Peace Moves

THE ALLIES were anxious to keep Stalin fighting Hitler's 'Barbarossa' armies, as the Russian losses had been catastrophic. Stalin was equally worried in case the Western Allies made a negotiated peace with Hitler. Crafty and devious, Stalin played cat-and-mouse throughout 1943 with Churchill and Roosevelt. In the same period Ribbentrop wanted to broker a peace with the Russians. In June, according to Basil Liddell Hart, he met the Soviet Foreign Minister, Molotov, at Kirovograd inside the German lines and other German intermediaries met Alexandrov, a senior Soviet official. When Hitler got to hear of these talks he dismissed them as a 'Jewish provocation'. After the huge tank battle at Kursk which exhausted the Germans, with Hitler's permission the intermediaries, Peter Kleist and Edgar Klauss were again encouraged. The sticking points seemed to be agreement on frontiers. Vladimir Dekanozov, a former Soviet ambassador and now Deputy Foreign Minister, had talks in September with Kleist in Stockholm. Ribbentrop's diary recalled, 'This time Hitler was not as obstinate as in the past. He walked over to a map and drew a demarcation on which he could compromise with the Russians.' Mussolini, now a refugee, having been rescued from Allied captivity in November, at Hitler's instigation, now arrived at Hitler's HQ. Hitler told the Duce that he wanted to settle with Russia, but he then said to Ribbentrop, 'You know if I settled with Russia today I would only come to blows with her again tomorrow – I just can't help it.' Stalin was in fact, quite serious. When, in May 1943, Churchill and Roosevelt postponed the invasion of Europe for a year, the Soviet leader was known to have been absolutely furious. He revealed the Klauss–Kleist meeting at the Teheran Conference in November to embarrass the Allies.

Prost!

A bottle of red *Führerwein*, bearing a label showing Hitler dressed smartly in suit and tie, was issued to top-ranking Nazi generals in 1943 to mark the Führer's fifty-fourth birthday. The separate neck label for the 12-degree alcoholic strength Schwarzer Tafelwein showed an eagle surmounting the Nazi swastika.

The Broken Treaties

GAULEITER ERICH KOCH of East Prussia – a friend of Göring's and *no* friend of Ribbentrop's – presented the latter after his successful visit to Moscow in August 1939 with a beautiful amber casket. It was given to 'the greatest European Foreign Minister since Bismarck' (according to Hitler), as something in which to preserve *all* the treaties that he (Ribbentrop) had signed on Hitler's behalf.

The Nazi–Soviet Pact was the eighteenth, of which seventeen were eventually broken. The only one not broken was the International Sugar Agreement – and that had been suspended at the outbreak of war in 1939. On Ribbentrop's fiftieth birthday in 1943 he was given another opulent casket adorned with semiprecious stones. It was empty. Hitler was convulsed with laughter.

Strychnine Poisoning

HITLER had a number of doctors, among them Brandt, Morell and Giesing. Morell had specialized since 1931 in diseases of the urinary system and in venereal diseases. He treated Hitler's meteorism (gas in the abdomen) with Dr Koster's Antigas Pills, sometimes up to sixteen a day. These did little good and in 1944

Dr Giesing discovered that these pills contained almost the maximum amount of strychnine – the Führer was being systematically poisoned. But Hitler's perverse reaction was to fire Giesing and continue with Morell, who was by all accounts a charlatan.

Our Long-Legged Slender Women

EARLY IN 1944 it was clear to Hitler that Germany had to recruit more than 4 million *new* workers for the immense manufacturing demands of armaments, munitions, submarines, aircraft, tanks and rockets. A major conference took place on 4 January with Keitel, Speer, Milch, Herbert Backe (the Agricultural Minister) and with Himmler and Fritz Sauckel (the manpower supremos). Italian forced labour could not be used as four new Italian divisions had been formed from the prisoners of war taken by Germans after Italy's surrender to the Allies in 1943. Hitler was most reluctant to use female workers, 'Our long-legged slender women' cannot be compared with the 'stocky primitive Russian women'. After four years of total war the fraus' and fraüleins' place was not in noisy factories. The fact that Britain, USA and Russia employed millions of women in factories or on the land carried no weight at all with Hitler's romantic views.

Speer the Pure Technician

THE BRITISH NEWSPAPER *The Observer* of 9 April 1944 carried an article about Speer, which he, rather courageously, showed to Hitler. Part of the article read:

> Speer is, in a sense, more important for Germany today than Hitler, Himmler, Göring, Goebbels, or the generals. They all

have, in a way, become the mere auxiliaries of the man who actually directs the giant power machine . . . Speer is not one of the flamboyant and picturesque Nazis . . . Much less than any of the other German leaders does he stand for anything particularly German or particularly Nazi . . . He [is] the pure technician, the classless bright young man without background . . . [and] this is their age; the Hitlers and Himmlers we may get rid of, but the Speers, whatever happens to this particular special man, will long be with us.

Hitler might well have thrown a tantrum and sent Speer to a concentration camp or worse. He read the long article carefully and handed it back to Speer without a word, but with respect.

The Unusual Birthday Party

HITLER'S FIFTY-FIFTH BIRTHDAY, on 20 April 1944, was celebrated in the Berghof with champagne and a *Geburtstagstisch* (birthday table) covered with presents. There were several unusual happenings. Blondi, Hitler's beloved dog, sang with his master – Hitler howled, the dog howled and the duet went on for much of the evening. Usually totally abstinent, Hitler sipped a very sweet white wine. Amongst the scores of presents for the Führer were cakes, chocolates, fruit and various other food products, which were all destroyed on Hitler's orders in case they had been poisoned. He no longer trusted the German *Hausfrauen* who had so adored him for fifteen years.

Medals Galore

MILITARY DICTATORSHIPS adore medals and decorations and the Third Reich was no exception. During Hitler's years of power, 1933–45, more than 450 political and civil decorations were created, many based on their Weimar and Imperial predecessors. In 1939 Hitler reinstated the Iron Cross for bravery with a First Class; the Knight's Cross (*Ritterkreuz*), with oak leaves, with oak leaves and swords, with oak leaves, swords and diamonds, and finally with golden oak leaves. Göring made sure that he received every possible decoration, including Italian medals. Hitler gave him – only him – a Grand Cross of the Iron Cross.

Political and civil awards included the Blood Order for the original participants of the Beer Hall putsch, the Eagle Shield of Germany for intellectual achievement, and the 1929 Nuremberg Party Day Badge. Hitler sometimes wore his Great War Iron Cross, which he had been awarded as a regimental messenger/ runner.

Hitler's Lucky Star

AT THE END OF JUNE 1944 the Third Reich was losing the war on three fronts – to the Russians in the east and to the Allies in Normandy, while the Luftwaffe had been swept from the skies. Hitler displayed steady nerves and an astonishing capacity for perseverance. Speer thought that the 'time of struggle', the *Kampfzeit,* with its many setbacks, had strengthened his will to continue the fight. In spite of his rapid ageing and constant illness (despite Dr Morell's treatment), by auto-suggestion Hitler made himself believe in ultimate victory. Perhaps his new, vicious V-weapons would do the trick; perhaps the Allies would fall out with each other. Although Hitler soberly understood the harsh military facts, Speer wrote that the Führer 'could not be shaken in his expectation that at the last moment Fate would suddenly turn the tide in his favour. If there was any fundamental insanity in Hitler, it was this unshakeable belief in his lucky star.'

Hitler and the Secret Weapons (2)

The most potentially valuable secret weapon developed by Willy
Messerschmitt in the Augsburg plant was the Me-262 fighter
(called the *Schwalbe*, 'Swallow'), with two *jet* engines, a speed of
over 500 mph and a fighting capacity superior to the Allied
fighters. The Me-262 was the first fully operational jet fighter,
well ahead of the Gloster Meteor.

Hitler, a Great War infantry soldier, could not see its potential
until in January 1944 he read an article about British success in
developing jet engines. So, with Speer's agreement, he ordered
Field Marshal Milch to increase production of the secret Me-262,
which could help destroy the American and British bombers.
But he was under a misapprehension – he thought the 262 was
being developed as a bomber, and Milch had to tell him that this
was not the case, quite late in its development. Speer, Jodl,
Guderian, Model, Dietrich, as well as Milch and all the
Luftwaffe generals, were adamant that the Me-262 was a superb
fighter aircraft, not a bomber. But Hitler thought he knew best
and insisted that it should be turned into a fighter-bomber – so a
system allowing it to carry two 250-kg bombs was hurriedly
lashed together. As an aircraft it was underpowered, its advanced
airframe far outstripping the development of its engines.
Although fast, it was not a very stable gun platform, its engines
were unreliable, and it was, like all turbojets before the
development of the afterburner, very slow to accelerate, with a
long take-off run. In the end, flak batteries and conventional (i.e.
piston-engined) fighters had to be deployed at airfields to
protect 262s during take-off. The engines tended to ignite tarmac
runways, so the aircraft were further restricted to airfields with
concrete runways. All in all, the 262 was insufficiently
developed; there were too few of the aircraft operational, and it
was tricky to fly, even for highly experienced pilots, while the

'HOUSE OF CARDS'

Hitler's European conquests fight back.

logistical problems of supplying and servicing the aircraft proved almost insurmountable. In addition, it came into service too late – the Allies had by now invaded Europe and thereby won almost complete domination in the air.

The Bomb Plot and *Blutrache*

COLONEL CLAUS PHILIPP MARIA SCHENK, Graf (Count) von Stauffenberg (1907–44), a brave soldier who been severely wounded in Tunisia, where he had lost a hand, was appointed Chief of Staff to Colonel-General Fritz Fromm. This presented a golden opportunity, for although a member of the largely pacifist Kreisau Circle, he was also leader of a widespread conspiracy to assassinate the 'Master of Vermin in the Third Reich', i.e. Hitler, and form a new government. At 12.10 p.m. on 20 July 1944 Stauffenberg, attending the Führer's daily conference in the Wolfsschanze, carefully placed a briefcase containing a time bomb under the table near Hitler and then left the room to make a phone call. Unfortunately, another officer probably then moved the briefcase to the other side of a solid oak table. Stauffenberg waited outside until, at 12.42, the time bomb blew up. There were a number of casualties, including four deaths, but Hitler survived, with his uniform in tatters, his ear drums burst, his right arm, legs, hands and face lacerated. That afternoon Mussolini and Marshal Graziani arrived for a scheduled meeting. Göring, Himmler, Ribbentrop and Admiral Dönitz attended and the witch-hunt for the conspirators started, with Goebbels and Himmler rounding up, by means of the dreaded Gestapo, anybody they thought might be involved. This operation was named *Blutrache* ('blood vengeance') by Himmler. Over 7,000 arrests were made and the Gestapo used diabolical torture to extract names and more names. Over time, almost 5,000 souls were executed (accounts vary as to the exact number); arrests and executions continued till the end of the Nazi era, many being arrested and executed on trumped-up charges, among them Graf von Moltke. Stauffenberg and the main army conspirators were shot, most of them within hours of the bombing; and as for many of the other executions – Goebbels sent cameramen to film them taking place. The famous Field Marshal Rommel committed suicide. Hitler, Dönitz and Göring addressed the nation on the radio. Hitler said, 'It was a crime without parallel in German history . . . I was spared a fate that holds no terror for me, but would have had terrible consequences for the German people. I regard this as a sign that I should continue the task imposed on me by Providence.'

Eva and Adolf – a Loving Couple

AFTER the Stauffenberg bomb assassination plot, Eva Braun wrote to Hitler in July 1944: 'Right after our very first meeting I promised myself I would follow you everywhere, even unto death. You know I live only for the love I can give you.' Hitler presented her with a book of poetry by Ludwig Thoma entitled *Josef Filsers gesamelter Briefwexel*. He inscribed it 'Meine liebe, Eva herzlichst Adolf Hitler, Berlin, an 19/Jan 1940,' which translates as 'My darling Eva. A gift of love from the heart.' Before her suicide in the Berlin bunker in May 1945 Eva made various bequests of her worldly goods, and this book went to her friend Herta Schneider. It is now valued at about £100,000.

Sippenhaft

HEINRICH HIMMLER, Hitler's appalling henchman, was one of the most powerful men in Nazi Germany. He had almost total physical control over Germany and the occupied territories; his SS and Gestapo were feared all round Europe for their savagery and brutality. It was Himmler who carried out the 'Final Solution' on his Führer's instructions. The word 'resettled' was a euphemism for extermination. He inspected some of the concentration camps and was responsible for planning methods of murder such as mobile gas vans. It is said that when he was present at a mass shooting of Jews, to his great distaste, his coat was splattered with brain matter; as a result he thought a 'more hygienic' method of killing should be used – this led to the gas chambers.

The many concentration and extermination camps were under his control, run by the *Totenkopfverbände* (Death's Head branch of the SS). His *Einsatzgruppen* SS special action groups, four units each of three thousand men, murdered about three-quarters of a million Jews and Russian political commissars in Russia. After the Stauffenberg July 1944 bomb plot failed Himmler reintroduced the medieval custom of *sippenhalf* or 'blood guilt', whereby treachery was deemed a manifestation of diseased blood, and thus the *entire* families of the suspected assassins or traitors must be exterminated.

On 22 May 1945 Himmler, a fugitive, was arrested by a British soldier in this author's divisional area around Flensberg in Schleswig-Holstein; the following day, before he could be interrogated, he used his cyanide pill to escape the hangman.

Nuclear Research, Stage 4

HITLER'S PRINCIPLE of scattering responsibility meant that scientific research teams in the Third Reich were divided and often at odds with each other. According to the 'office journal' of 17 August 1944, not only all three branches of the armed forces, but also the SS and even the postal system had *separate* research facilities. Thus progress on the development of nuclear fission was negligible. In the USA all the atomic physicists were grouped in one organization. Speer, the Minister for Armaments, had 2,200 recorded points and subjects in his conferences with

Hitler. Nuclear fission came up once – Führer Protocol 23 June 1942, Point 15. Of course the Great War soldier was less likely to want to understand the awful potential that led to Hiroshima.

A Tavern in the Town

ALOIS HITLER, half-brother of the Nazi dictator of Germany, ran a pub in the great square of the Wittenbergerplatz in Berlin. He was remembered as 'a harmless-enough fellow, grown portly on good beer, whose chief fear was that his half-brother would fly into a rage and order him to close shop, since the Führer did not like to have people reminded of the lower-middle-class origins of the Hitler family.' Abstinent as he was, the Führer was unlikely to approve of a tavern in the family.

Eva's Treasures

HITLER WAS, by his standards, very generous to Eva Braun. Initially he bought her medium-priced jewellery and in 1932, three years after meeting her in the photographer Hoffman's studio, an apartment on Munich's Wiedenmayer Strasse. For her twenty-first birthday he gave her a matching set of ring, earrings and bracelet of tourmalines. It remained her favourite jewellery. Then he bought a house in Munich for Eva and her sister Gretl at 12 Wasserburgstrasse, and in March 1936 a Mercedes car and driver. Soon Eva was buying handmade Italian shoes, dresses by Fraülein Helse, a Berlin couturier, silk underwear from Paris and sports outfits from Vienna. Hitler was also generous to Gretl and he gave Fritz, Eva's father, a gold watch and a dog on his sixty-fifth birthday. In her will, dated 24 October 1944, Eva listed fifty pieces of jewellery, many containing emeralds, diamonds, rubies, beryls, sapphires and gold, and a dozen fur coats, including one of sable, and another of mink.

Hitler's 'Wacht am Rhein'

TOWARDS THE END of November 1944 Hitler made it plain to his key henchmen that 'Wacht am Rhein', the codename for the great December counter-attack in the Ardennes, was his last effort. He told Speer, 'This will be the great blow which must succeed. If it does not succeed, I no longer see any possibility for ending the war well . . . But we will come through. A single breakthrough on the Western Front! You'll see! It will lead to collapse and panic among the Americans. We'll drive right through their middle and take Antwerp. Then they'll have lost their supply port. And a tremendous pocket will encircle the entire English army, with hundreds of thousands of prisoners. As we used to do in Russia!'

Secretly, three huge armies, two of them SS, unleashed a terrific onslaught in mid-December. Fog, mist and snow kept the Allied air forces grounded. Savage fighting between the disorganized Americans and Hitler's armies around St Vith and Bastogne lasted until late January 1945. The American General Patton wrote in his diary, 'We can still lose this war,' and Churchill was forced to ask Joseph Stalin in Moscow to bring forward his spring offensive. It was touch and go. Hitler had masterminded a huge secret offensive – known to the Allies as the 'Battle of the Bulge' – that not even Bletchley Park's ULTRA operation could detect.

Permanent Euphoria

NEW YEAR'S EVE 1944 found Hitler and his entourage of adjutants, doctors, secretaries and Bormann, of course, drinking champagne. Hitler's western HQ, from which he had been directing the Ardennes offensive, was a series of bunkers, camouflaged as blockhouses, hidden in woods at the end of a grassy valley near Bad Nauheim, just north of Ziegenberg. The audacious drive from the Ardennes to seize Antwerp was noticeably failing. But Hitler, as usual, was making optimistic forecasts for the New Year. 'In the end we will be victorious,' he declared to his circle, who took these prophecies in silence. The alcohol had relaxed everyone but the atmosphere was very subdued. Hitler was the only one who seemed to be drunk without having taken any alcoholic drink; Albert Speer wrote that he was in the grip of a permanent euphoria.

Atom Bombs Against Britain?

HITLER did sometimes comment on the prospects of nuclear fission. He was not happy with the possibility that the Third Reich might be transformed into a glowing star and joked that the scientists in their urge to uncover all the secrets under Heaven might some day set the globe on fire. But he was confident that he would certainly not be alive to see it. Speer was certain that Hitler would not have hesitated for a moment to employ atom bombs against Britain.

The Nuclear Story – a Near-Run Thing

DRESDEN WAS BATTERED and burned between 13 and 15 February 1945 by the RAF and the USAAF. Hitler was beside himself with fury and spoke to Dr Giesing in the Berlin Chancellery. 'I'm going to start using my Victory weapon [*Siegwaffe*] and then the war will come to a glorious end. Some time ago we solved the problem of nuclear fission and we have developed it so far that we can exploit the energy for armaments purposes [*Rüstungszwecke*]. They won't even know what hit them! It's the weapon of the future. With it Germany's future is assured.' Albert Speer had visited the Krupp armaments works and was shown parts of Germany's first cyclotron. And at

Heidelberg in the summer of 1944 he was shown 'our first cyclotron splitting an atomic nucleus' by Professor Walter Bothe. Professor Walther Gerlach was the Reich chief of nuclear research trying to finalize the research work done by Professors Werner Heisenberg and Carl Friedrich von Weizsäcker. They had started in 1939 and were developing an experimental atomic pile at Haigerloch. So Hitler's boast – ten weeks before the end of the Third Reich – was perfectly valid.

Frederick the Great – Hitler's Hero

IN 1934 Hitler purchased an oil painting of Frederick the Great by Anton Graff for 34,000 marks – a huge sum. It travelled with him everywhere. His *Chefpilot* Hans Bauer ensured that, packed in a special bulky crate, handled with care, it travelled in the Führer's plane with precedence over other passengers. Rochus Misch, a telephone operator in Hitler's bunker, recalled, 'Very late one night I went into the study. There was Der Chef gazing at the painting by candlelight, sitting there motionless, his chin buried in his hand, as if he were in a trance. Hitler was staring at the King [Frederick]. The King seemed to be staring right back . . . It was like stumbling upon someone at prayer.' In *Hitler's Table Talk* Frederick II of Prussia is mentioned admiringly twenty-two times. 'When one reflects that Frederick the Great held out against forces twelve times greater than his, one gets the impression: "What a grand fellow he must have been!"'

Shortly before his suicide in the bunker Hitler gave the painting to Bauer as a parting gift.

Germany – 'a Wasteland'

IN THE LAST FEW MONTHS of countdown to *Götterdämmerung* – the term so often applied to the end of the Third Reich – Hitler sent out several decrees (the first was on 19 March) ordering a 'scorched earth' policy: the destruction of factories, bridges, radio stations, railway tracks, canal locks, locomotives, passenger carriages, freight wagons, cargo vessels and barges. Rivers and canals would be blocked by sinking ships in them. Every type of explosive and ammunition would be used. The last decree, dated 29 March 1945, read, 'Aim is creation of a transportation wasteland in abandoned [surrendered] territory.' Hitler had previously ordered the commanders of all the Channel port fortresses (Brest, St Malo, Cherbourg, Calais, Boulogne, Le Havre, Ostend, Zeebrugge and the Scheldt harbours) to ensure the total destruction of these ports on surrender. This had been done, but the destruction had been outside Germany. Now Hitler had ordered the same thing to happen to his own country, in Operation Nero. It was only due to Albert Speer's constant intervention, risking his neck in the process, that the Hitler edict was watered down and in most cases, ignored. Speer made a long, brilliant speech on the radio on 16 April, which undoubtedly prevented further damage to the infrastructure of Germany.

Hitler's Miracle?

ON 12 APRIL 1945 the American President Roosevelt, architect of Allied victory together with Winston Churchill and Joseph Stalin, died. Goebbels, listening to American news agencies, was first to hear it and telephoned Hitler in excitement. In the Berlin command bunker a delighted Adolf Hitler, with considerable animation, shouted out to the entourage (Bormann, Ley, Schaub and other adjutants and orderlies). Some remained dubious until Hitler received the news agency report. He held up the paper. 'Here, read it! You never wanted to believe it. Here we have the miracle I always predicted! Who was right? The war isn't lost. Read it! Roosevelt is dead!'

Goebbels and the other henchmen were bubbling over with delight. Their Führer was convinced the tide would turn. History was repeating itself. The hopelessly beaten Frederick the Great had won a last-minute victory; the House of Brandenburg had been granted a last-minute miracle. Innumerable fantasies burgeoned in the bunker as the group of defeated Nazi leaders clutched at straws. Perhaps Mr Truman, the new American President, would wave a magic wand of honourable peace.

A few weeks later Stalin's Russian hordes overwhelmed Berlin. There was no miracle.

The Isle of the Departed

IN THE LAST WEEKS of his life in the Berlin bunker, Hitler gave the impression of a man whose whole purpose in life had been destroyed. He was shrivelling up like an old man. His limbs trembled and his signature on papers and decrees was illegible. He walked with a stoop and dragging footsteps. His voice quavered. The old masterful Hitler had vanished. Speer recalled that his tantrums were no longer childish but those of an old man. His complexion was sallow, his face swollen. His uniform, which had always been scrupulously clean and tidy, was now dirty and stained with food. He was diminished and appeared senile. His three cronies towards the end were the faithful Martin Bormann, Goebbels and Robert Ley. He was still touchingly fond of his long-serving secretaries, Frau Wolf and Frau Schröder, and also of Traudl Junge, the widow of an SS officer who had died in combat in 1944. On 22 April, he ordered many members of his inner circle and his staff to leave the bunker, including Frau Schröder and Frau Wolf, and Dr Morell. Eva Braun had determined to be with her man at the finish. And Goebbels had declared, 'My wife and family are not to survive me. The Americans would only coach them to make propaganda against me.' The discipline in Hitler's entourage had gone and it was like a tomb in the concrete bunker, isolated from the appalling tragedies as the Russians smashed their way into Berlin. In Speer's words the unreal world of the Hitler bunker was the 'isle of the departed'.

Letter from the Bunker

On 23 April 1945 Hitler admitted to Ribbentrop that the war was lost, and dictated to him four secret negotiation points to put to the British. If the European continent was to survive against Bolshevik domination then Germany and Britain 'must bury the hatchet'. He ordered Ribbentrop to write immediately and secretly to Churchill. 'You will see. My spirit will arise from the grave. One day people will see that I was right.' This letter to Churchill was circulated as a memorandum to the British Cabinet. Churchill also sent the letter to Stalin on 12 July 1945, saying, 'It is exceptionally long and tedious.' Hitler had said to Ribbentrop, 'I actually came to power ten years too soon. Another ten years and I would have kneaded the Party into shape.' In their last discussion the Führer, quite calmly, stated that he had never wanted any harm to come to Britain. The big handshake with 'Germanic' England – that had always been his goal.

Chocolate Cake and Puppies

In the final days in the bunker Hitler gave orders to the troops trying to defend Berlin, rarely allowing any retreat. He appointed officers, sacked others, had some executed. It was a dream world as the Russian bombardment thundered down. The Führer ate immense quantities of chocolate cake and played with Blondi and her five puppies who lived in one of the bunker's bathrooms. It is almost certain, judging by Hitler's mood swings, that his doctor, Morell, himself probably a morphine addict, had been injecting his Führer with morphine (and he left a provision behind when he departed from the bunker). Eva Braun, meanwhile, fantasized about starring in a movie based on her life.

Speer's Farewell

ALBERT SPEER determined to see Hitler one last time in the Berlin bunker as the Soviets reached the suburbs. With the city under constant Soviet attack, his plane landed by the Brandenburg Gate. 'Was that to be the end of our many [twelve] years of association? For many days, month after month, we had sat together over our joint [architectural] plans, almost like co-workers and friends. For many years he had received my family and me at Obersalzberg and had shown himself a friendly, often solicitous host.' Speer had an emotional bond with his Führer, who had promoted him to the highest levels of authority in the Reich. Bormann and Adjutant Schaub greeted Speer. They wanted him to advise Hitler to get out of Berlin, fly to Berchtesgaden and take over command in South Germany, and Hitler did in fact ask Speer for advice on two key issues. The first question was whether he should stay in Berlin or move out. Speer answered, 'End your life here in the capital as Führer.' The second question, surprisingly, was who should be Hitler's successor. Speer thought that Admiral Dönitz was infinitely preferable to Herman Göring, the deputy Führer, or to Goebbels or Martin Bormann, and advised Hitler that the Admiral would be the best choice. In any case, Bormann promptly sabotaged Göring's claim, and both Goebbels and Himmler would commit suicide. The Admiral was the Reich President for three weeks in Flensberg, and the government was nicknamed the 'operetta government'.

Hitler's 'Travel Marshal'

JULIUS SCHAUB was Hitler's personal servant and part of the Osteria Bavaria social circle. He negotiated 'fees' for Hitler at NSDAP meetings and rallies. The 'fees' were paid as 'expenses'. Schaub was described as 'chief adjutant', and shortly after his master's assumption of power he took over responsibility for Hitler's tax affairs, all his travel arrangements and all the day-to-day monetary needs. Finally, Schaub guarded Hitler's private papers. Having served time in Landsberg prison with his master, Schaub was a dedicated, loyal servant who was eventually made an SS Colonel-General (Obergruppenführer) and ADC to the Führer. He took part in the 'blood purge' of the SA alongside Hitler and was also his bodyguard, chauffeur and valet for over twenty years, services rewarded with a legacy in Hitler's will of 1938. The Hitler circle nicknamed Schaub the *Reisemarschall*, *Reise* meaning 'travel'. Eventually, immediately before Hitler's suicide in the bunker, Schaub destroyed most, perhaps all, of Hitler's personal papers in the Chancellery garden. He himself left the bunker on the night of 25–6 April and was sent to the Berghof to destroy the rest of his master's papers. He arrived there drunk, to hand over a letter from Eva to her sister Gretl. All his world had been destroyed. What did he have to live for? But live he did, until 1967.

Hitler's Personal Testament

AT MIDNIGHT ON 28 APRIL in the Führerbunker, Hitler began dictating to his secretary Traudl Junge: 'During my years of struggle, I believed I ought not to engage in marriage; but now my mortal span is at its end, I have resolved to take as my wife [EB] who came to this city when it was already under siege, after long years of true friendship, to link her fate with my own. It is her wish to go with me to her death as my wife. This will make up for all I could not give her because of my work on behalf of my people.'

His will, after naming Martin Bormann as his executor, ended, 'I myself and my wife choose death to escape the disgrace of being forced to resign or surrender. It is our wish to be cremated immediately at the place where I have done the greatest part of my work during the twelve years of service to my people.' It was witnessed by Joseph Goebbels, Martin Bormann and Colonel Nicolaus von Below, another of Hitler's adjutants.

The Political Testament

IN CONTRAST, Hitler's political testament, which listed the Fuhrer's appointments to the new Cabinet and expelled Göring and Himmler, was on the whole a rambling blend of *Mein Kampf* and his *Second Book*. Traudl Junge later wrote, 'I thought how undignified it all was. Just the same phrases, in the same quiet tone and then, at the end of it, those terrible words about the Jews. After all the despair, all the suffering, not one word of sorrow, of compassion. I remember thinking, he has left us with nothing. A nothing.'

Dated 29 April 1945, 4 a.m., the political testament was witnessed by Joseph Goebbels, Wilhelm Burgdorf, Martin Bormann, and General Hans Krebs.

Four copies of both witnessed documents were entrusted to his adjutant and press chief. For a few hours, by deed of Hitler's will, he was succeeded as Reich Chancellor by Paul Joseph Goebbels.

The Wedding in the Bunker

HITLER HAD DILLY-DALLIED with Eva Braun since October 1929. She had been his loyal friend, rarely his lover, rarely his confidante, but had given him her total devotion for almost sixteen years. She came to join him and, as she was well aware, to die in the Berlin Führerbunker. Dressed in her elegant navy-blue dress embroidered with sequins and Ferragamo black suede shoes she married her strange, dying Führer. Walter Wagner, a Berlin municipal councillor, was deputed to conduct the civil ceremony. It was three o'clock in the morning. The witnesses were Goebbels and Bormann (whom Eva hated). Hitler and Eva declared that they were both of pure Aryan descent and not affected by incurable diseases that would exclude them from marriage. To add to the tension of the moment Wagner signed his name 'Waagner', and the bride started to write her surname with a B, then crossed it out and signed 'Eva Hitler née Braun'. A funereal champagne reception followed, with few friends, no music, no flowers, and only thirty-six hours left to live.

Champagne in the Bunker

HITLER'S DEATH WAS IMMINENT. 'I have resolved to stay here . . . I shall not fight personally. There is always the danger that I would only be wounded and fall into the hands of the Russians alive. I don't want my enemies to disgrace my body either. I've given orders that I be cremated. Fraülein Braun wants to depart this life with me, and I'll shoot Blondi [his dog] beforehand. Believe me, Speer, it is easy for me to end my life. A brief moment and I'm freed of everything, liberated from this painful existence.' Later, towards midnight, Eva Braun sent an SS orderly to invite Speer, who had been almost a confidant over the years, to have a drink with Hitler. 'How about a bottle of champagne for our farewell? And some sweets? I'm sure you haven't eaten in a long time.' So Moët et Chandon it was, with cake and sweets, and the two chatted away about Goebbels, Bormann and the Russians. At three o'clock on the morning of 30 April Speer said farewell to his Führer, who simply said, 'So, you're leaving? Good. *Auf Wiedersehen.*' Hitler retired to bed at four a.m.

Later that day, after a light lunch, Hitler bade farewell to his inner circle and to members of staff. He and Eva then retired to his study. In an outer chamber clustered members of the old guard – among them, Bormann, Goebbels, Artur Axmann (founder and official of the Hitler Youth), Ambassador Hewel, Hitler's adjutant Otto Günsche, his valet Heinz Linge and his chauffeur Erich Kempka. Soon after, in the little green and white study, Eva Hitler crushed and swallowed her cyanide pill and her husband put the 7.65 mm Walther pistol in his mouth, bit his capsule, fired and died. *Götterdämmerung* had come and gone.

Martin Bormann's Death

AFTER THE BODIES of Hitler, Eva Braun, Goebbels and his wife Magda (who had just murdered her six children) were doused with petrol and set alight by SS guards, there was a helterskelter rush for the door by most of the survivors. Three of them, General Hans Krebs, General Wilhelm Burgdorf and SS Hauptsturmführer Schedle stayed behind and shot themselves. Some escaped, mostly to be captured sooner or later; a few others, including the telephonist Rochus Jordan Misch, who is still alive, Traudl Junge and a nurse, Erna Flegel, were among those who stayed in the bunker to be captured by the Russians. Martin Bormann and Hitler's physician Ludwig Stumpfegger escaped – but no great distance: they got as far as Lehrter railway station, came under Russian fire, were wounded and took their cyanide capsules. Their bodies were buried under the rubble and were not discovered and identified until many years later. For decades, however, rumours abounded concerning Bormann, with flight to South America as a possibility.

Hitler's Death

ON 1 MAY 1945 at a political dinner party with Churchill, Lord Beaverbrook, Oliver Lyttelton and others, Jock Colville brought in the sensational announcement broadcast by Nazi wireless that Hitler had been killed at his post in the Reich Chancellery in Berlin and that Admiral Dönitz was taking his place. It was thought that Hitler might have been dead for several days, but 1 May was a symbolic date in the Nazi calendar and no doubt the circumstances ('fighting with his last breath against Bolshevism') were carefully invented with an eye to the future Hitler myth and legend. Churchill thought that Hitler was perfectly right to die as he had.

The End of the Third Reich

THE RUMP OF HITLER'S THIRD REICH, Grand Admiral Karl Dönitz's Flensberg government, was holed up in the massive Schloss Glücksburg. At 10 a.m. on 23 May 1945 the British division in which the author served – 11th Armoured – was tasked with the capture of all the members of this interim government in Flensberg. The 15/19th Hussars, 1st Battalion Cheshires and 1st Battalion Herefords swept into the Schloss. Dönitz, Jodl, Speer and a number of minor politicians were captured and handed over to US General Rooks's mission from SHAEF (Supreme Headquarters Allied Expeditionary Force). Only Admiral Hans von Friedburg crushed his phial of cyanide. The Reich war flag, raised every day at the naval school, was

'PEP TALK TO THE DEAD'

lowered by the British troops. These – and the Nuremberg War Crimes trials – were the last stages of the Third Reich.

Hitler the Painter (4)

IN 1983 DR AUGUST PRIESACK, a Munich art authority, and the US collector Billy F. Price jointly published a catalogue of Hitler paintings. Many of the so-called 'Hitler' paintings are forgeries by a German artist named Konrad Kujau, author of the notorious 'Hitler diaries'.

In September 2006, an auction of twenty-one paintings and two sketches attributed to Adolf Hitler realized £118,000. They were discovered in 1986 in a Belgian attic, and had been painted by Hitler some seventy years before. *The Church of Preux-au-Bois* sold for £10,500, *Church at Louvignies* for £6,000, *A Row of Cottages* for £5,500 and a double-sided watercolour canvas depicting an airfield on one side and a landscape on the reverse went for £3,500.

The Marquess of Bath has a collection of thirty of Hitler's paintings at Longleat and there is another collection at the Imperial War Museum, London. One of these is entitled *Church and Village of Ardoye in Flanders, summer of 1917.*

Eva Braun's Art Collection

OBVIOUSLY FUNDED by Hitler, Eva Braun possessed a significant art collection: landscapes by Fischbach, Baskon, Midgard, Wax, Gradl, others by Gallegos and Franke, and portraits by Rosl, Popp and Hugo Kauffmann. Eva's favourites were a watercolour by Hitler, *The Asam Church*, a portrait of Hitler by Bohnenberger and a north Italian landscape by Bamberger. Hitler gave her a painting from the 'school' of Titian which Mussolini had given him. Others in the collection included a portrait of the Führer by Knirr, a portrait of Eva by Bohnenberger, a landscape of Rimini, some old watercolours of Venice and canvases by Tiedgen, Hoberg, Krauss and Hengeler Hilbakt. The fate of this collection is not known.

Hitler's Huge Purchases of Art

ONE OF HITLER'S KEENEST AMBITIONS was to plan and endow a huge art complex with a museum in his favourite home town of Linz. During 1943 and 1944 he purchased some three thousand paintings at a cost of 150 million Reichsmarks. A further 8 million Reichsmarks were spent in the last twelve months of the war. In late 1945 American troops found 6,755 paintings owned by Hitler in the salt mines of Alt-Ausee, destined for the Linz museum.

GLOSSARY

Deutsche Arbeitsfront (DAF) German Labour Front
Deutsche Arbeiter Partei (DAP) German Workers' Party in Germany
Einsatzgruppen ('task forces', 'intervention groups') paramilitary groups operated by the SS
Ermächtigungsgesetz ('Law to Relieve the Distress of the People and Reich') Enabling Act of 23 March 1933 that allowed Hitler and his cabinet to enact laws without the participation of the *Reichstag*.
Forschungsamt (FA) Nazi intelligence services
Four-Year Plan economic reforms created by the Nazi Party.
Freikorps ('Free Corps') far-right paramilitary organizations
Gau a NSDAP (Nazi Party) regional district
Gauleiter a Nazi Party leader of a Gau
Gestapo contraction of **Ge**heime **Sta**atspolizei: 'secret state police'
Kristallnacht the 'Night of Broken Glass', 9–10 November 1938, when Jewish businesses were attacked by violent mobs
NSDAP, Nationals**o**zialistische Deutsche Arbeiterpartei (National Socialist German Workers' Party), better known as the Nazi Party
Obergruppenführer ('Senior Group Leader'), second highest rank in the SS
Reich Empire, realm
Reich Chancellery office of the German Chancellor
Reichsführer the highest rank of the SS, with only a single holder, Himmler
Reichsleiter ('Leader of the Realm') the second highest political rank of the Nazi Party, the highest being Führer
Reichstag Germany's parliament; the building in which it met
Schutzstaffel (SS) ('protective squadron'), large security and military organization of the Nazi Party
Sturmabteilung (SA) Storm (Assault) Section of the National Socialist movement
Waffen-SS ('Armed SS') the combat arm of the Schutzstaffel
Wehrmacht 'Defence force' Nazi Germany's armed forces 1935–45

SELECT BIBLIOGRAPHY

Allen, P., *Crown and Swastika* (Robert Hale, 1983)

Allen, M., *Himmler's Secret War* (Robson, 2005)

Bullock, A., *Hitler: A Study in Tyranny* (Penguin, 1967)

Conradi, P., *Hitler's Piano Player* (Gerald Duckworth & Co., 2005)

Gun, Nerin E., *Eva Braun* (Meredith Press, 1968)

Heiden, K., *The Führer* (Carroll & Graf, 1999)

Hitler, A., *Mein Kampf* (Hurst & Blackett, 1939)

Hitler, A., *Second Book* (Enigma, 2003)

Irons, R., *Hitler's Terror Weapons,* (Collins, 2002)

Jörgensen, C., *Hitler's Espionage Machine* (Lyons Press, 2004)

Junge, T., *Until the Final Hour* (Orion, 2003)

Kershaw, I., *Hitler – Hubris* (Penguin, 2001)

Kershaw, I., *Hitler – Nemesis* (Penguin, 2001)

Lambert, A., *The Lost Life of Eva Braun* (Century, 2006)

Liddell Hart, B. H., *The Other Side of the Hill* (Cassell, 1951)

Nicolson, N. (ed.), *Harold Nicolson: Diaries and Letters 1930–1939* (Collins, 1967)

Reuth, R. G., *Goebbels* (Constable, 1993)

Schad, M., *Hitler's Spy Princess* (Sutton, 2004)

Shirer, W. L., *The Nightmare Years 1930–1940* (Birlinn, 1984)

Speer, A., *Inside the Third Reich* (Sphere, 1971)

Taylor, J. and Shaw, W., *Dictionary of the Third Reich* (Penguin, 1997)

Trevor-Roper, H. (ed.) *Hitler's Table Talk (1941–44)* (Weidenfeld & Nicolson, 1953)

Whetton, C., *Hitler's Fortune* (Pen and Sword, 2004)